Thomas W. Shane, DDiv

When Life Meets Death
Stories of Death and Dying, Truth and Courage

"**W**hen death comes in the many violent, unexpected ways Tom Shane has seen, it can be almost unbearably painful. It would be totally unbearable were it not for the support given by people like Shane who generously and skillfully offer their services to the victims left behind in the tragedies—the survivors. It is to these individuals (from the bombing of the Murrah Federal Building in Oklahoma City to the victim of a single-vehicle accident) that support must be given so life can go on.

Shane recounts some powerful stories, but his most powerful message for all of us is that we must be present for one another when life meets death. This book is must reading for caregivers."

Thomas A. Welk, DMin
*Director of Education,
Hospice Incorporated,
Wichita, KS*

"**T**om Shane writes with unusual skill in describing his many years of working closely with the implications of death for the dying. Further, he describes the implications for public safety officers, hospital workers, clergy, and others who struggle to maintain life, but who are forced to deal with those critical moments when life hangs in the balance.

Shane's stories of death and dying are profoundly tied to the emotions of the living as well as confronting the realities of the dying. His stories are gripping because he has been there and has felt personally what he is describing."

Merrill F. Raber, PhD
Psychotherapist in private practice,
Behavioral Science faculty member,
Via Christi Family Practice Residency,
Wichita, KS

"**C**haplain Supervisor Thomas Shane invites the reader into more than a storytelling, and certainly more than a 'teaching moment.' His brief vignettes are a sharp rap on the heart, inviting, challenging, and haunting us into a deeper reality, where we sit next to the pain of grief, the numbness of loss, the paradox of violence and love. We are invited to savor small helpings inside the deeply human moments of loss, death, and grief.

These small stories' power is often nearly overwhelming, and yet we can catch a luminous hope that invites faith, even in the midst of deep darkness. Shane's personal experience as a chaplain to disaster opens wide our senses to see, to hear, to smell, to taste, and to feel the real wounds of the spirit. He most clearly knows, and wants us to know, the power of remaining faithful to the task of soul-healing. There is much for reflection in these pages, which should be shared and savored in small portions.

Those seeking to understand the faithful movement of persons into the broken moments of life will discover in Tom Shane a companion seeker whose courage and clear purpose inspire those just entering into caregiving work, and more experienced hands as well."

Fred L. Smoot, PhD
Anchor Chaplain, Psychiatry,
Barnes Jewish Hospital,
Washington University Medical
Center, St. Louis, MO

"Tom Shane's book, *When Life Meets Death*, brought back many stored moments of emotion. Moving beyond the details, facts, and figures surrounding death, Shane writes of the human experience at the end of life, from the perspective of the 'front lines.' He takes the reader to the heart of the matter, to the essence of why death matters—how it is a threshold through which we all must pass, as loved one, as care provider, or as participant. Somehow, Shane has been able to discuss the utter despair, fear, and tragedy of death, and yet reminds us that we are human, that death is real and cannot be escaped, that the loss hurts terribly bad, and that death can be an experience surrounded by a beauty and dignity unmatched by any other human endeavor.

Anyone who has ever been a parent, had a parent, faced the death of a loved one, or faces their own death should read this book. Even for a 'tough' grown man who tries to hide emotion, it pierced my heart with thoughts of my parents, my family, my patients, . . . my own destiny. One word of advice for the 'tough guys.' Read it alone."

Curtis B. Pickert, MD
Columbia Wesley Medical Center
Wichita, KS

"Thomas Shane reminds, as much as teaches, all caregivers of truths encountered in ministering in the midst of death and dying: of lost hopes and dreams; of the cost of hearing the other's story; that healing is a communal event; that there are moments too raw for words; that presence or standing with the other is our human calling; that hope is frequently forged only in the rubble of our lives; that in listening to stories of suffering we are on 'holy ground.'

These truths are captured with special poignancy in stories that describe the dying of Shane's own parents and his involvement with the rescue workers at the Murrah Federal Building in Oklahoma City.

I recommend this book to those who, without abandoning the viewpoint of objective science, understand the fundamental power of story to trouble our minds, break our hearts, and lead us to truths that mend and redeem."

James D. Daugherty, ThD
Director of Pastoral Care,
Supervisor of Clinical Pastoral
Education, Christian Hospital
Northeast-Northwest,
St. Louis, MO

The Haworth Press, Inc.

When Life Meets Death
Stories of Death and Dying, Truth and Courage

THE HAWORTH PRESS
New, Recent, and Forthcoming Titles
of Related Interest

A Memoir of a Pastoral Counseling Practice by Robert L. Menz

When Life Meets Death: Stories of Death and Dying, Truth and Courage by Thomas W. Shane

The Heart of Pastoral Counseling: Healing Through Relationship, Revised Edition by Richard Dayringer

The Eight Masks of Men: A Practical Guide in Spiritual Growth for Men of the Christian Faith by Frederick G. Grosse

Hidden Addictions: A Pastoral Response to the Abuse of Legal Drugs by Bridget Clare McKeever

When Life Meets Death
Stories of Death and Dying, Truth and Courage

Thomas W. Shane, DDiv

The Haworth Press
New York • London

The Haworth Press, Inc., 10 Alice Street, Binghamton, NY 13904-1580

Cover design by Marylouise E. Doyle.

Library of Congress Cataloging-in-Publication Data

Shane, Thomas W.
  When life meets death : stories of death and dying, truth and courage / Thomas W. Shane.
     p.   cm.
  Includes index.
  ISBN 0-7890-0289-2 (alk. paper).
  1. Death–Psychological aspects–Case studies. I. Title.
BF789.D4S455 1997
259'.6–dc21   97-19562
                                                                            CIP

In memory of my parents,
Jack William Shane
Alma Grace Shane

ABOUT THE AUTHOR

Thomas William Shane, DDiv, is Chaplain Supervisor at the Columbia Wesley Medical Center in Wichita, Kansas and Adjunct Instructor at Hutchinson Community College, where he teaches classes on ethics and death and dying. Prior to joining the staff at Columbia Wesley, he was a Chaplain Supervisor at Prairie View, Inc. He is a regular columnist for *The Newton Kansan* and *The Kansas Trooper* and is a consultant to local churches and Harvey County, Kansas Emergency Services for critical incident stress management. Dr. Shane is a Board Certified member of the College of Chaplains, a Certified Professional Mental Health Clergy member, and a former president of the Kansas Association of Chaplains.

CONTENTS

Acknowledgments

To work with persons involved in the dying process is to work inside a Holy Moment. It is to witness another's last good-bye and to feel one's own remembered sorrow for the losses in one's life. One must do this work with a kind heart and an awareness of one's own faithful center. Above all else, one must encounter those in grief with respect. Indeed, for a moment in time, they have opened their broken hearts to be touched with help and healing.

I wish to thank the many anonymous people who allowed me to enter their lives in their time of sorrow as they approached death. It is their stories that I tell in this book. However, I have modified personal details and circumstances to protect the privacy of those with whom I have worked. For some, death was expected. For others, death was a sudden, unexpected, and unwelcome intrusion. Some were my own family members; most were strangers. All of them shared their story with me and thereby enriched my life.

I wish to thank Kim Hollinger who patiently prepared the manuscript for publication. I also extend thanks to my colleagues in the Pastoral Care and Education Department at Columbia Wesley Medical Center who have offered friendship, support, and wisdom.

Finally, I am grateful to my wife, Linda; my children, Kim, Mark, Mike, and Sara; and my grandson, Lee, for their willingness to understand my inclination to attend to the world of the deeply troubled person. My love for them is woven into the fabric of all my caring.

* * *

I gratefully acknowledge the permission of Prairie View, Inc., to reprint a revised form of a brief summary of grief responses that I previously prepared for them.

Grateful acknowledgment is also made to the following publications for permission to reprint the stories listed, which appeared there in a slightly altered form:

The Newton Kansan

When Disease Ravages a Child
Often a Child Just Wants to Be Heard
Hats, Sheriff Badges, and Sticky Fingers
Christmas "as Usual" Seems So Empty
Life's Timetable Is Beyond Our Control
Teddy Bears and Fluffy Blankets: A Child's Bill of Rights
A Smile Hides the Pain of Dreams Gone Astray
More Yesterdays to See Than Tomorrows
Trust Even When Fog Shrouds Your Vision
I'm Still Walking Home with My Dad
A Splendid Teacher for a Difficult Lesson
Pieces of Pineapple
Holding Hands Until the End
When Life and Death Hover Together
Children Are to Be Loved, Not Hit
When Tomorrow Comes Too Soon
The Loss That Has No Equal
Death Strips Away the Veneer
With the Gentleness of the Setting Sun
Sandwiched Between Joy and Sorrow
Finding Hope in the Midst of Suffering
When Tears Say What Words Cannot
Unleashing Memories from the Past
A Broken City
How Are You? What Was It Like?
Returning to the Scene of an Evil Act
Memories Shared at a Table
All of Us Hurt When One of Us Hurts
Elusive as the Prairie Wind
Grief Binds Us in Silent Kinship
What Matters Most Is That We Are Loved
Visiting with a Few Old Memories
To Be Healed, Pain Must Be Shared

The Kansas Trooper

The Unknown Samaritan
A Killing Combination
A Season Out of Time
Stan Smith's Brother
Between Chaos and Coffee
Nothing to Do
Healing the Helpers
Supermarket Homicide
Stone Cold Dead
It Hurts Too Much to Go On
Just a Recluse

Introduction

There are any number of ways to tell the truth about life, but no way is more common, yet powerful, than the use of story. Stories have always been the way people have kept their traditions alive and told others who they are. Perhaps the most important gift any of us have to offer others is our own story. Our story is our life. When we hear the stories of others we find a resonance with our own life stories and we understand their lives in ways we might otherwise never have known.

Our stories are holy. Through them we catch glimpses of truths that are redemptive and healing. But in these days, we seem to rely so much on science and technology that we forget the power of story. Science and objectivity have their place, but stories are the traditional ways that ordinary people speak of meaning and truth.

Stories capture the mystery of life, and they are crafted with the raw experiences of life: tears, laughter, warm hugs, and lonely good-byes.

All of us know so much more than our thinking, our reason, our knowledge will ever let us know. Stories are about the shadows and the mysteries of life as much as that which is made clear by science and technology. Stories help us know that which is real but which is elusive and slips away even as we seek to grasp it. Stories address matters and moments too deep for words. Stories are indirect ways to capture truth and meaning. In a strange way, the power of a story is less that we tell it, and more that it captures us. Stories disarm us so that truth and wisdom find natural ways to enter our hearts and our souls. Stories heal us even as they call forth our sorrow.

Some truths can never be adequately captured with the precision of science and research. Though factually accurate, they will always seem barren. There are some human experiences that are too deep for words; only the majesty of a story can illuminate their meaning. Some truths cannot be directly told, lest they fall to the earth and wither.

The moment of death is such a time and a form of truth that comes to mind. There is, of course, always a scientific explanation of death. A disease process or an accident has prompted certain biological realities to be altered so that life is no longer a possibility for someone. We can verify that death has occurred, how it came about, and when it happened. We need this kind of truth.

But death is never solely a scientific reality. Death marks the end of how one life was intricately woven into the lives of many others. Death is the end of dreams and joy. Death means no more hugs from a loved one. This kind of truth is recorded in the stories we tell about the one who died.

This book looks at the experience of death prior to the moment of death, at the moment when death occurs, the time following death, and occasions when death is traumatic. Indeed, there are many books on death and dying. What sets my work apart is that my writing is not instructional or theoretical in nature as are so many books on the subject. It relies, instead, on telling stories about this experience. The stories I tell are authentic, having their origin sometimes in the lives of people with whom I work and sometimes in my own life. I write about the raw edge of life and destiny even as hope and faith are inherent within each story.

I try to avoid what I believe to be a trite interpretation of the *meaning* of the story. If well told, the story itself makes the point. My intent is to invite the reader to enter the world of another person who is facing the death of a loved one. I want the reader to absorb the moment; to feel the hot tears of grief roll down cheeks; to experience from the inside out what this emotion is like. Stories can do that.

I believe the moment of death is at once spiritual, awesome, and terrifying. If it sometimes brings relief, it also brings great sadness. The most we generally allow ourselves to acknowledge is a tepid intellectual awareness of it. I strive for something deeper. The stories I tell are stripped of politeness and are my attempts to relay authentic experiences of ordinary people who have just endured a transforming event—the death of a loved one.

The stories about death that follow are not objective truths about death so much as they are tales about the meaning and the mystery of people who must face the death of someone they love. Read them with compassion, for indeed you are overhearing something holy.

PART I:
ON THE WAY

Every living thing will someday die; there are no exceptions. The only variables are when and how death will occur.

At some level, all of us know this, and we spend our lives with this reality always setting things in perspective. For the most part, we don't ruminate on our inevitable death so much as we intellectually acknowledge that it will happen . . . someday. Having an abstract awareness of this inevitability, however, is a safer, detached approach to our death. It remains an *idea* more than a *reality*.

It may be that this detached awareness serves a useful purpose. If we were to dwell on the fact that we will inevitably die, it seems likely that we would not embrace life with much joy and enthusiasm. More than likely, we would meet each day with dread and anxiety wondering if *this* would be the day of our death. Life would not hold much joy if we worried over our inevitable death with the same intensity that most of us do when we are given the diagnosis that we have an incurable illness and have only a short time to live.

Facing death is something like facing the sun. For a moment we can peer into its brilliant glow, but inevitably we must turn away because it is blinding and painful. So we turn aside and acknowledge that it is there and that it makes a difference in our days. Still, we don't focus so intently on it that we see nothing else. Indeed, to do so would itself be injurious.

Inevitable as death is, and though we generally keep a safe distance from it so that we can engage life with joy, there comes a moment in time when our intellectual awareness becomes a personal, terrifying experience. At that time, what had previously been an abstract, though certain, potential becomes an existential reality for us or for a loved one.

Indeed, if sometimes death is a friend because it promises the end of our debilitating decline, or an end to our sorrow and suffering, or a release from our present struggles, it is still, likely as not, terrifying. It marks the end of all we know and all we have been. It demands that we say our final good-bye to all whom we love. All that we once took for granted now seems threatened.

The reality of our death usually brings a measure of suffering to us. If modern medicine enables us to control the pain of the dying process better than in generations past, it does little to comfort and alleviate the suffering of those in the dying process. The fears of the dying are still very real.

So with a certainty that is unyielding, we move from knowing that *potentially* we will die, to a *crisis* knowing that our time to die has begun. If for some this change occurs in an instant because of some catastrophe such as an automobile accident, for others it is a process that lasts for a long while. A prolonged, incurable illness is such a fate.

Such people enter the world of science and technology where the magic of medicine and surgery prolong the inevitable, but do not stop it. Indeed, such persons continue to live even as they are dying. If there are moments of respite and hope, still the last corner of the journey has been turned and the end is in sight.

The time prior to death is marked by moments of great majesty. Ordinary though they are, these moments become markers. We see the inevitability of the impending death of a loved one and it becomes crystallized in a moment in time. In these moments, we see the bedrock issues of our humanity laid bare.

The stories that follow are about just such ordinary times. All are snapshots of the time prior to death when perhaps for the first time, the truth of this final reality is evident and the sacredness of life is made clear. This is the time when death is on the way and is as inevitable as the setting sun. Perhaps the stories that follow will call forth your own memory of a similar time in your life and you will taste your tears again or feel a smile cross your face once more as you remember.

When Disease Ravages a Child

Christina sat in the corner of her room. She scrunched as far back in the chair as she could with her chin resting behind her knees as if she were hiding. Sometimes she smiles, but mostly she is quiet and looks at me with stoic eyes. On most days she watches TV or works jigsaw puzzles. She doesn't let many strangers into her eight-year-old life. I can hardly blame her. Strangers mean well, but they offer procedures and surgery and the help they promise seems to hurt so much. She tolerates me. Once in a while we talk about "things." Usually I just get an accepting glance and a passive "hello" wave.

Her bright red hair hung to her shoulders on this day. It hasn't started to fall out yet. That will happen sometime soon when the ravages of chemotherapy take hold. That's one of the devastating consequences. Kids walk around the pediatric unit with baseball caps or scarves on their heads as a way to cover the obvious consequences of cancer and chemotherapy. Such beautiful children. There are no secrets here.

While she watched a favorite cartoon and her two brothers played a table game, I visited with her young mother. "I'd like to wait until Monday to talk to her. I want her to try to have a good weekend. Surgery isn't until Thursday and I have decided that that's enough time. Will you help me? I don't know what to say." She forced a grateful smile but her eyes glistened with tears that were ready to spill down her cheeks. Of course I would help, but already I felt my own insides tighten. I forced a smile, too. Each surgery seems riskier and this time it may not even work. Christina may not survive. Her family has decided she needs to know that this one is the riskiest of all. How do you tell your child that the surgery is essential, but so serious that she may die? My heart aches for this family. I don't want to think about the possibility of her death. It seems too devastating.

I glanced at Christina as she sat silently in her chair. Illness had robbed her of vitality and her thin arms hugged her knees as she seemed focused on the cartoons. She has been in and out of the pediatric unit and the intensive care unit for weeks. I know her family well. She is no longer a stranger to whom I offer care. She is a child from a family I am very fond of. I hate to see her come back because each time it seems that she loses ground. I cannot deny my own sadness at her decline.

Soon two nurses came in and one said to her mom, "We need to take the NG (nasogastric) tube out. The doctor said it's closed off and Christina isn't getting the food she needs. He said we would try regular feeding for awhile. She's *got* to eat, though, or we'll have to put another one in."

Mom gave a meek approval then covered her eyes. "I just can't watch this," she said as her face flushed. You can only watch your child suffer for so long before your own limits are stretched beyond resiliency, even when the procedure is quick and painless. With the announcement made, the nurses turned quickly toward Christina to do their job. Remembering other procedures, the little child pulled back in dread, but before she could react in terror, the tube was out.

For this tiny moment, there was joy; Christina smiled. In its own way this incident seemed so enlightening to me. A beautiful child, through no fault of her own, has been ravaged by disease. She seems to fail week by week. The most splendid minds we have can't stop the dreadful onslaught of illness. Each day I come to this family to bring them some comfort, perhaps a word of hope. I try to listen as Mom shares the anguish of her heart. There is not enough love to turn back the assault of this illness. I find some comfort in my daily discovery that whatever happens, this child has been loved. And with each downward drift, the steadfastness of her parents' presence makes the promise of their love even more secure. And every day I feel the anger in my heart that these children have to suffer so.

I don't know what will happen to Christina. Maybe the magic of medicine will grant another unexpected miracle. It has happened before. I'd like to see this child laugh, belly deep and loud. I'd like to see her plump and happy and surrounded by school friends who celebrate her ordinariness and not her illness. I'd give a lot if her mother could talk to me in the years to come about how difficult it is to raise a teenage daughter and not, on this day, about how agonizing it is to watch her child die by inches. I spend every day with people who are filled with passion and courage. Much of my work is with bald-headed kids who smile at me. It's just that some goodbyes hurt so much.

Often a Child Just Wants to Be Heard

"Hi, Aaron. It's Tom. How are you today?" I said as I greeted the child. It's hard to know how children with leukemia are doing. So many factors determine what makes a good day. Has the treatment made them sick? Is this an extra stay in the hospital because of a fever? Have they had to miss a school activity because of a relapse? After awhile you get to know the children fairly well and even before they say a word, you sense the state of their soul. It's not magic; it's just that you learn to read all the subtle ways they communicate. They can come in and out of the hospital so many times that soon, you learn how to interpret the subtle signs in their behavior that hint of unspoken truths. It's important to attend to these.

Sometimes a child's body communicates a truth long before the child has words to use. In fact, they may be telling you things they don't even understand themselves. Like today. Though Aaron is usually active, on this day he is subdued. Chemotherapy has stolen his hair so he wears a red bandanna and a black, hooded sweatshirt. Everyone knows it's to cover his bald head. Even so, masquerade though it is, it affords him a way to manage the reality that the road to wellness is through some barren places. It isn't just vanity that causes him to wear the head covering. That's too easy an explanation. It is that his baldness makes it public that he is afflicted with an illness which is potentially lethal and it sets him apart. He covers his head so he doesn't have to face this truth every minute of his life.

I watched him as I greeted him and felt my heart turn on edge. The spark in his eyes was gone, replaced by what seemed to be resignation. Or fear, maybe. His covers were pulled tightly up to his head so that only his face showed. He looked like a mummy.

"So, Aaron, how are you today?" I asked again.

"Not too good," he replied.

If kids deserve their privacy and their right to keep to themselves, they also deserve the opportunity to share their story and find support. But those who would listen must be prepared for the cost.

"Well, Aaron, you look kind of worried today."

"Well, yeah," he replied. "I am."

"If you want to tell me about it, I'll listen."

From out of the shroud of blankets Aaron looked at me with his eleven-year-old perspective and confided in me, "I'm afraid. I have to have surgery. I need to have a port-a-cath put in so they can get to my veins and I'm afraid that I may die in surgery. That can happen, you know. You can die from surgery." He paused and looked me squarely in my face as he continued on. "And I'm also afraid that I'll die of leukemia, anyway."

It was quiet in his room. In his own direct, trusting way, Aaron told me why it was he was buried under his blankets inside his darkened room. Some days are too hard to live; some words too hard to say. And hope is sometimes too elusive to grasp when you live at the edge of life itself. I could not imagine how lonely his world must be. My heart ached for him. I wanted to hold him and promise him that it would be OK. I wanted to take away his dread, but I could not. I could only listen.

I tried to encourage him to talk to his doctor or nurse so that he could have the most accurate information about the surgery which, as such things go, is considered routine. But Aaron's wisdom was deeper than mine. He took me at my word and trusted me with the truth of his soul. He lives each day under the specter that he may die too young, too unfairly.

"The doctors just want to talk to me about surgery and how it will go. They don't want to listen to me about how I feel and that I'm afraid. Nobody listens to that."

For a moment in time this child believed in me and trusted me. He took me at my word and told me about the deepest truth of his life. He invited me to listen to his dread and his terror. He didn't ask me to fix anything or to talk to anyone else for him. Quite simply, he asked only to be heard and for me to sit with him in the deep, thick darkness of his fear and to offer him my willingness to do nothing at all but sit . . . and listen . . . and care.

Some children are not in touch with their own anxiety. Others who are refuse to share it, as if keeping it locked up will contain it and give them some mastery over it. But once in a while I meet an

Aaron who is wise beyond his age and trusting beyond his experience. Such a child bids me to slow down and listen.

"You still have those pictures of your fishing trip?" he asked me in a little while, needing to find a new place to focus.

"They are in my office. Want to see them?" I replied.

"Yes," he said as a smile brightened his face. You can only look into the abyss of fear for so long and then its time to reach for whatever hope and possibility there is to grasp.

Hats, Sheriff Badges, and Sticky Fingers

Luke sat in the middle of the bed with a large brown castle in front of him. Sometimes it was hard to find the kid in the middle of all the toys piled around him. A green alligator with its mouth wide open lay right beside a long silver shark. His favorite toy seemed to be the Transformer . . . a man that can be transformed at the press of a button into a mythical creature with wings and obvious super powers. I couldn't help but wonder if the thought ever crossed his young mind how splendid it would be if he could be a Transformer and with the press of a button become so strong that he could soar into the heavens and conquer all evil at will—even his childhood cancer. With the attention span of any five-year-old, Luke played for a while with his Transformer and the other animals, trucks, cars, and GI Joes only then to shift attention to the movie on the TV.

Just in front of him, his nurse, Kim, administered medication into the catheter that was inserted into his body. He seemed nearly oblivious to her work although he sneaked a look at her as she lifted his shirt, uncapped the needle and inserted it into the catheter line. It contained the magic medicine that promised him hope.

When your life evolves around leukemia, the idea of "normal" takes on a completely different meaning. Maybe that is because always nearby is the IVAC machine and the bag of magic medicine steadily dripping fluid into the plastic tubing which feeds into his tiny body as a constant reminder that life for him is lived with different rules.

I watched Luke from the doorway of his room waiting my turn to visit. All the children in the Peds (Pediatric) Unit are precious, but upon occasion it happens that one of them finds a way into the secret place in my heart. I let very few in, but all of a sudden they are there. I can't explain it. It unsettles me. I am not even sure how they get there. I try carefully to make certain that everyone gets what they need. But one day I knew that this child was at home in my heart.

Seeing me in the doorway, his mother said, "Luke, look who's here." His eyes brightened and his face broke into a grin. This sick child pointed a finger at me and said, "Tom! Are you coming to my party? It's Thursday at three o'clock. It's my last treatment! Come early!!"

I sat on the chair beside his bed and for awhile we played with the toys. Then, remembering his great secret, he said, "Mom, show Tom my hat!" From a suitcase the great treasure was carefully removed and placed on his head. I know about hats. Hats aren't just head coverings. They are signatures; they fit the person, and this hat was Luke. It was old, bent, sweat-covered and frayed. It wasn't all shiny and slicked up like some store-bought new piece of clothing with no class at all. Not on your life. This one had character. When he placed it on his head, the drawstring went immediately into his mouth and he began to chew on it. Right smack dab in the middle of the crown was a heavy, silver star which read, "Special Deputy." Luke knew how to wear it. Tilted just slightly backward, the star shone brightly and the hat sat there as if it belonged, which, of course, it did. Luke wore his hat with pride.

Someday I'll be assigned to another unit or I'll decide I need to do something else with other patients. There may come a time when the cost of living this close to sorrow on the Pediatric Unit is a price I choose to pay no longer. But not for awhile. Every day I sit on the floor or on a bed and let some sick kid touch my life. Every day Luke smiles at me and is glad that I am there. For awhile we talked about the things that make life important. We talk about hats and sheriff badges and Transformers and chocolate cakes. He tells me how he and his dad go fishing and how sometimes they catch turtles and about rattlesnakes in glass cages at the shop where his dad works.

Every day I learn about how to face horror with a smile. Every day I learn what it really means to trust someone with your very life, comfort, and destiny. Every day I come to bless a child and come away blessed myself. And every day I see how splendid is each unfolding moment and how it can never come again and must be celebrated for the ordinary gift it really is.

Luke's party to celebrate his last inpatient chemotherapy treatment was a grand affair. His mom and dad were there along with two other leukemia kids and their moms and lots of nurses. We ate chocolate cupcakes.When it was over, I shook his chocolate-covered (and slightly sticky) hand good-bye and walked down the hall.

Christmas "as Usual" Seems So Empty

He seemed so tiny in the crib and he made no sound at all. I wanted to touch him—to hold him, really—but I didn't. The heart monitors on his chest and the intubation tube that let him breathe made it sadly clear that this child, only hours old, was too fragile to hold. I could only be present and hope that all my prayers and the power of my spirit would convey the truth that I was there, along with my love, and trust that that would suffice. I didn't want him to be alone.

I turned away from the nurses. I didn't want to share my anguish with them for personal reasons. They might have wanted to offer comfort, but I preferred the silence of the evening halls at Wesley where I could walk alone and hide behind my badge and be a staff member, not a new grandparent whose soul was filled with anger and sorrow, both at once.

Only hours earlier that which should have been a moment of majesty, the birth of our first grandchild, turned into an episode of horror. I am still confused about *how* it happened and will struggle forever with *why* it happened, but must accept that it happened. But it has left me battered and reeling. As a theologian I struggle to find meaning and comfort in this event which seems both senseless and brutal.

The expected normal birth of this child suddenly turned into an emergency caesarean section when an unexpected and unpredictable medical episode changed everything. Within minutes the wonder of new life was transformed into wondering if life would survive at all.

The child was born without a heartbeat and had to be revived before he ever had a start. All of last week was spent grasping for even tiny pieces of good news. There were some. There were no seizures. He was off the ventilator within hours. He was of a reasonable size. The MRI was negative. Indeed, all indications so far are favorable. But nothing denies the truth that he had to overcome great

13

odds to even be here at all. Mother and child are home now. His mom and dad are intent on finding a normal life.

But we all live with the haunting dread that some catastrophic and silent malady awaits in the darkness of each unfolding developmental task in light of his precarious start. We hardly speak our dread: that this precious child possibly suffered a silent injury from lack of oxygen.

And so we wait. Already the days seem endless and we watch each move that he makes and pray for every sign of normalcy. We smile at one another and give thanks for every apparent good sign. But our smiles cover our tears. Some truth will take years to be fully known. We will have to learn to be content with each day that unfolds and to not see ghosts in the shadows where none exist.

All across the land it is Christmastime. Everywhere lights brighten homes and new holiday cards from old friends arrive telling stories of last year's joy and how life changes. We have some presents already purchased.

But it doesn't feel much like Christmas to me. This year, I just want the season to pass. Advent is a time of waiting and preparation. But in our house we wait and prepare for signs that a tiny new life will be healthy and whole. It is not the season to be jolly.

Christmas as usual seems empty and I don't find any joy in the sign of hope that even in the worst of times . . . and maybe because of the worst of times . . . God is silently present in our lives, then that is the only truth of Christmas that I care to celebrate. But it is a hard truth I hold in my head while my heart feels mostly bewilderment.

And so I wait. I want all that is ordinary and dull and normal and usually overlooked, but which holds within it the essence of Good News: a baby crying loudly for food. A child who learns to look longingly for his mother when he hears her voice. Eyes that see. A heart that beats. A child who sits. Tantrums and the "Terrible Twos." Clear thinking and crisp words.

But this is Advent, and I must wait for the good news.

Life's Timetable Is Beyond Our Control

Ever so gently the young mother unwrapped the receiving blanket so that she might look carefully at her new baby boy. She caressed his tiny head and kissed his cheek. Little David lay as still as a whisper while a breathing machine worked his lungs. His little fingers were all properly formed and curled into a tiny fist.

"What are those little lines in his fingers?" she asked the nurse who stood beside her holding a handful of tubes that fed the oxygen into his prematurely born body. "Because he was born so early his skin is still transparent and those are his veins," the nurse said in a gentle voice. I thought she sounded sad. Just beside us another nurse set up a portable screen to give some privacy to the mother and child in this fragile moment.

Born just hours ago and several months too soon, the infant hovered in a hazy twilight zone somewhere between life and eternity. Tiny tubes fed oxygen and other medical magic into his frail body in hopes that it would be enough to sustain his life until he would be strong enough to make it on his own.

I sat next to the mother who held little David in her arms. Overhead the heat lamp warmed the space until I felt uncomfortable with the heat. I knew from the physician's report that in spite of all this effort, it was a losing battle. But sometimes the effort is offered as much to care as it is to cure. I listened with a weariness in my heart as the young mother said to baby David, "Come on, David. You've got to get well for your two big sisters."

All parents desperately hope that the life that springs forth from their love for one another will be enough to carry their child to vibrancy. Every newborn life carries with it the silent hopes of the parents that yesterday's mistakes will find resolution with this sweet child and that this child will somehow miraculously walk unscathed through life's hard times.

But it was not to be. Life has limits and unfolds in a timetable beyond our control or understanding. Beyond our love or deepest yearnings every life will ultimately yield to the relentless forces of life and death. And so it was for little David.

Even as we prepared to leave so that baby David could receive more care, my pager summoned me to the Coronary Care Unit. "Code Blue. CCU West. Room 304." Already the family had gathered when I arrived. A deep stillness settled over the room. Standing in the company of their family, each member stood quietly and alone. Muffled weeping broke the silence. Here and there someone blew a nose in a tissue. Eyes red from grief looked fondly at the nearby ninety-year-old patriarch who had said his final good-bye and now lay as silent as yesterday. How amazing that even as a body grows cold in death, the power of the life still warms the hearts of those who loved him.

I put my hand on the shoulder of the ancient widow who sat hunched over in her wheelchair beside the bed. She grabbed my hand and held on. "Sixty-five years," she said with a smile. "We've been married sixty-five years. This day has come too soon. I wish it could have lasted forever." I sucked back my own tears so I could talk. "I'm sorry for your loss, but I am happy you have such treasured memories," I said to her.

Two people. One day. Such different experiences. Each one profoundly touched my life. Little David came into life too early and died too soon. He was probably unaware of anything in his brief twelve hours of life. Nevertheless, he was loved. Even barely lived lives touch us. They remind us of fresh hope and possibility and how we must care for one another because in some strange way we belong to each other.

And even ninety-year-old deaths have an edge of sadness. If we could hear but one more of their stories and have one more chance to talk with them . . . but still that wouldn't be enough. There is never enough time with those we love.

Life is precious. It is ours but for a fleeting moment and then it fades like a dream upon waking. Each life matters, whether one is too young to understand one's own reality or too old to work anymore.

I work in a place where this occurs, yet I scarcely understand. Perhaps it is enough that I stand in awe of the mystery that surrounds me with each person I meet.

Teddy Bears and Fluffy Blankets:
A Child's Bill of Rights

It was quiet in the Pediatric Intensive Care Unit. The nurse gently applied a fresh dressing to the child's head. The warming blanket, spread carefully across the child, was pink and fluffy. A teddy bear sat beside her and kept its own silent vigil as if it hoped the child would wake from her deep coma and hold it in her arms as once she had done. A tiny intubation tube was inserted into the child's mouth and rhythmically forced air into her fragile lungs, keeping her connected to life . . . or at least some minimal existence.

Only hours before, the bedside scene was a frenzy of medical magic. Surgeons stood vigil beside the child. Pediatricians took note and stood ready to assist. Pediatric residents watched intently and tried to learn how the science of medicine is also an art of care. Nurses and respiratory therapists offered their wisdom, too. Always, the tiny child lay still. She was lost somewhere between life as we know it and her eternal destiny. We could see her body but the vibrant soul that once made her so alive seemed to slip farther away.

No amount of love or science can undo the devastation of a bullet to and through the brain. There are times when the best of our minds and the most precise skills we can muster fall victim to the evil of our violent society. The consequences of some atrocities simply cannot be undone. One more beautiful child has paid the price for the sinful, wicked horror of those whose blind rage knows no compassion or judgment. Once again, a child has paid the ultimate price when adults resort to violence to resolve their disputes. Shame on them for their violent ways.

I cannot tell if I am filled more with sadness or anger. I stand at the bedside of a child so beautifully created in God's wisdom and see her tiny features so delicately and perfectly crafted. I see her splendid beauty utterly devastated by a vicious gunshot wound to the head—the innocent victim of a gangland drive-by shooting. I am filled with horror. How many more children must die a vicious death because some adults do not have the capacity to resolve their conflicts with wisdom?

It is not just a child who died here; it was *trust* itself. It would appear that children cannot trust that they will be born into a world that will love them and help them build their dreams. Children have a right to security and a life of hope. They have a right to sit in the laps of those who love them and listen to their stories. Children should never have to be cared for by strangers who barely know their names in places filled with noise and needles and suffer pain which never ends and experience fear which shatters the spirit.

Children have a right to be held in arms that love them and will hold them tight on stormy nights and tell them that though the thunder is loud, it will go away. They should not have to hear the thunder of weapons and feel the instant crunch of a bullet as it cracks their skull and destroys their brain matter so that even if they live at all, they will forever exist in a shadowy world of broken bodies and broken dreams. Children have a right to lay on the grass and watch fluffy clouds form never-ending pictures in blue skies. They have a right to sit around campfires at night and tell ghost stories which send tingles of delight up and down their spines. They don't have a right to have their spines shattered by violence so that they never walk, never talk, or never play again. Children have a right to frolic on snowy afternoons and build snowmen and flop on their backs and make snow angels. They should not have to prematurely meet an angel who welcomes them too soon to eternity because of the vengeful act of some adult.

Someday soon, I will watch another mother stand in horror, tears washing down her cheeks as she hears the doctors say, "I am sorry. We have completed the brain flow study and there is no more brain activity. There is nothing else we can do. Your child is dead."

Once more I will hear the mournful wail of grandparents who grieve the loss of their grandchild even as they watch helplessly while their own child shudders in grief at the untimely death of her baby.

When that happens, for one more time I watch the grief-stricken adults stand in apprehension around the bedside as machines are disconnected and monitors grow silent and the vigil comes to an end. I will be surrounded, again, with a deep silence as thick and consuming as ever I know. I will watch teary-eyed nurses remove the intravenous lines and wrap the child in fresh blankets for final viewing.

I will hear a physician respond to my question, "How are you doing?" with a clenched jaw as he says, "OK, thanks for asking," and turn away from me lest I see through his eyes clear down into his soul where he stores one more memory of one more child and one more shooting and one more fruitless medical effort.

God help us.

The Unknown Samaritan

I walked up the steep embankment to the accident site where an unknown traveler knelt beside the victim. With an expertise that seemed natural, she pressed on his chest, then tried to breathe life into the critically injured victim. I stood by in awe at the willingness of the stranger to touch the nearly lifeless victim. It takes courage to run this kind of risk today. Disease and lawsuits are the new reality for helpers. Back and forth she rocked as she knelt by his side in a widening pool of blood. I stood nearby as yellow-coated paramedics arrived. One began to cut the jeans off the victim. Another started an IV. Another applied an air bag to his mouth. All the while the stranger pressed his chest in a steady rhythm. The unknown victim lay silent with his vacant eyes peering past the stranger and the paramedics into a distant world seen only by him. And what did he see? The horror of the past moment? A reality beyond this life that is only seen by those summoned to a life after death?

Soon enough the gathering band of paramedics began to take over the care of the stranger. The good samaritan, an unknown woman who tried her best to stave off death, quietly withdrew from the scene and melted into the crowd. From somewhere she had donned a pair of latex gloves to offer herself some protection. Her clothing was, nevertheless, stained a bright crimson, giving notice to all the world that she had knelt at the very edge between life and death and was marked by her efforts.

I watched as she carefully pulled off one glove, then folded it deftly into the other as she removed it, too, and then tossed them both on the shoulder of the road as if she had done this kind of thing before. But her forearms and knees were bright red. Gloves were not enough to completely protect her. Some traumas are so raw that no matter where you are or how you protect yourself, you will be stained with the consequences. That includes blood as well as sorrow.

Not many folks have such an encounter. It is neither life nor death, but rather a twilight existence between time as we know it and destiny, and one does not know which way life will turn. For awhile, another's life is sustained because your own hands beat for their heart and your own breath fills their lungs with possibility. Given half a chance to consider the risks, most of us would turn away. Or at least wait long enough to ensure that all the safety precautions were in place: gloves, air bag, protective clothing, eye shields. After all, we have our families to think about and our own life to consider. Who can blame a good samaritan for doing what is sensible?

But sometimes good samaritans throw caution to the wind and act anyway. Is it out of ignorance of the risk? Or is it because unless one acts now, the wounded victim will surely die and the samaritan decides to accept the personal risk in spite of good judgment? Or maybe there is no thoughtful consideration at all, only a response borne out of compassion because the one before you is so mortally wounded, that unless you act, he will surely die.

And then she was gone. No one got her name in the frenzy of the situation. She asked for nothing in return for her effort. Like the good samaritan of long ago, she reached out to a helpless stranger, then vanished. I wonder what it was she thought about in those frantic seconds.

Once upon a time we would have called this long-haired, alcohol-smelling male victim a hippie. Or a drunk. Or something worse. But there he was, regardless of appearance, sprawled in the dead center of a Kansas country road on a bridge with his head caved in, his body broken in many places, lying in a thickening pool of his own blood. And kneeling beside him was a stranger, covered with his blood, trying as best she could to press back the onrushing force of death as it nipped at the victim's life like a pack of hungry prairie coyotes.

There on the yellow line in the center of a country road, the silent victim lay while the paramedics provided emergency care, hoping they would offer enough magic to keep him on this side of life. If he were to live at all, it would likely be in part because a passerby stopped and helped. Some of us are paid to help. Training, equipment, and experience give us an edge. We accept the risks, but we do so with safeguards on our side. But once in a while, a stranger happens by and lends a hand.

Not far away, the LifeWATCH helicopter landed in a nearby field. A cloud of dry prairie dust swirled about and stung my face. With heads bent low, the paramedics loaded the victim into the helicopter. The big engines melted into the wind and a great quiet settled over the prairie. In the silence of the prairie, it was my time to look at the human dimension of the tragedy.

When the paramedics are hard at work seeking to save a victim, and when the jaws of life fill the air with their deafening roar, when the helicopter lands so close by that bits of sod sting your face there is too much confusion to think. But when it is over, the ordinary items cry out to be noticed.

Two bright red roses separately wrapped in clear plastic cellophane lay between pieces of shattered windshield. They appeared to be gifts from the victim to brighten the day of a loved one. And then, as if they were nothing but debris, they were scooped up and tossed away with other trash onto the flat bed of the wrecker. Dreams are so easily broken and thrown away.

The blood-splattered eyeglasses of the young passenger lay unbent and unbroken on the highway as if they had been carefully laid down. I picked them up and placed them in the ambulance as the young woman was transported to a local hospital.

A while later, I stood in the treatment room with the trooper as we confirmed the expected message to the passenger; the driver did not survive his massive wounds. As the trooper conveyed the truth to the woman, she said she understood. Perhaps she did, but I wonder.

And then it was over. There was nothing left but memories. I wonder what became of the traveling good samaritan who appeared on the highway, immersed herself in the center of the trauma, and then vanished. Though her labor was in vain, her care and courage touched all who saw her. I still see her hard at work on the highway. Did she know her work was fruitless? But then again, some things are done because of the rewards they *might* bring. Maybe I needed to know that there are still some strangers who care enough for others to get involved and ask nothing in return.

And who will never receive the roses? Who will never receive the love of the one who tumbled from life into eternity in a twinkling of an eye after he was thrown from the vehicle?

I left the scene and went home. The warm winter evening seemed enchanting. The red sun was slipping behind the prairie at the edge of town where I live. It didn't seem to be a day for sorrow. It should have been a day for sunsets and red roses and laughter.

A Killing Combination

"Can you move your toes?" asked the doctor. The trauma team surrounded the injured man on the gurney, each one busy at some task designed to bring as much healing and hope as possible to the injured patient. Not getting any response from the patient, the doctor tried again. "Can you feel this?" she asked, touching the patient's feet. I watched her face as she did her work. She seemed attentive to every detail and carried herself with the confidence of a young, well-trained senior surgical resident.

But even surgeons have feelings hidden deep within their presented professional faces, and I saw a look of sorrow in her eyes. Leaving the patient, she walked to the X-ray screen, on which a series of films told the bitter truth. The radiologist pointed his pen at the one critical film which showed the spinal column with a severe separation. In a hushed voice he told the resident, "His spinal column is severed. If he lives, I'm afraid he'll be a quad." With that, he shook his head and walked away.

I finished gathering my information and left the trauma room as the patient was wheeled to surgery to stabilize his critical injury.

A trooper stood nearby and handed me the patient's driver's license as he said, "Unfortunately for him, this one looks pretty clear. We've got a witness. He ran a stop sign and T-boned the other car. He was speeding and never slowed down. When he comes out of surgery and sobers up, he's going to have to deal with being a quad and having killed a passenger in the other car. Booze and speed. It's a combination that kills. Everybody lost with this one."

I nodded in agreement. How sad, I thought to myself. For everyone. One victim was dead. One victim will be a quadriplegic—if he lives. Two families were involved, and each one will be devastated and spend a lifetime trying to adjust to this radical and unwelcome reality. And it was all preventable–that's what left me so sad. One life was lost, one life was shattered, and two families were devastated.

Sometime soon, the wife and parents of the patient will arrive at my hospital and have to face the bitter truth of this tragedy. It will be my job to tell them what happened. This is the part of my work I detest: bringing bitter news to good people that will change them forever. For a moment in time, I will be immersed in their anger and sadness as they pour out their grief and anguish. And when all is said and done, the tragedy will still be there.

Although some of my work is as a police chaplain, much of my professional time is spent as a hospital chaplain. I wear two hats. Because I have two professional identities, I work both sides of the same street. Sometimes I work on the scene with the troopers, while other times I work in the hospital emergency department when the traumas arrive.

Perhaps if the people could see the sorrow of the patients' eyes and hear the despair in their voices, as I do, when they learn that they have done something which will leave them forever paralyzed, they might change their own behavior. If they could see a young wife when she learns that her alcohol-impaired husband will never walk again and their dreams are now shattered beyond repair, perhaps they might think twice about drinking and driving or driving with reckless speed. If they could see a young mother broken and bent in a cold stubble field, thrown from her car because she didn't wear her seat belt, maybe they would be more careful. Then again, perhaps it wouldn't make any difference at all. How sad. But it all matters to me, because I must too often tell another family the worst news they will ever hear.

A Smile Hides the Pain
of Dreams Gone Astray

His face carries a smile that breaks into a laugh quicker than anyone I know. Tall and handsome, his gray beard and tweed sports coat make him look like the professor he really is. When I saw him leave the dining room and walk toward me, he looked like the Phil I'd always known. As I stood next to him, I felt sad at what I believed to be the marks of age and weariness that I saw on his face. He seemed weathered and worn. His eyes were still bright and eager enough, but they were surrounded by lines that showed signs of wear. He no longer used a cane but with two knee replacements, he was a little more cautious and slightly stiff when he walked.

I wasn't surprised, of course. After all, my own joints tell me every day that whether I like it or not, time moves on and parts of me slow down, too. Still, I wished for the old days when more of life was there for all of us to enjoy. As we stood together at the top of the stairway at the seminary and talked, I remembered the days gone by and how important Phil has been to me.

He was one of the first to encourage me to become a supervisor. I remembered the conference in Kansas City when he played the piano and we all stood around and sang every old song we could remember. Once, another supervisor told of how Phil refused a position he was offered so she, the runner-up, could have it because it just seemed the right thing to do. Phil passed it off with his trademark laugh and twinkle. Phil always laughs a lot when in the presence of a compliment or a sad memory, or when someone tells of his having done something gracious and they praise him.

"So, Phil, how's your wife?" I asked. Phil looked at me straight on as he said, "Not so good. She's in for another round of chemo this week. Makes her feel terrible. The good thing is, it's the kind of cancer that responds to treatment; the bad thing is, it's spread so far."

And with that, ever true to his nature, Phil chuckled as if to say nothing was too bad to knock him down and went right on to say, "The darn thing is, I'm at retirement age. But if she dies, all those plans we had made together won't happen. It wouldn't be the same without Delores. Just wouldn't be the same."

Phil smiled. At least his mouth smiled; but his eyes didn't brighten and the twinkle was dim. Eyes tell secrets that words can't name and laughter masquerades.

"Maybe I'll just keep on teaching. I'll need something to do. I still have lots of ideas. I still want to get a group of two or three topnotch students and a couple of other supervisors and go to someplace like Guatemala and work there for awhile." Phil brightened up when he looked beyond the chaos to some far distant possibility. But we both knew how deep a pit needed to be crossed before that dream could be realized.

I have heard chuckles when it hurts and seen eyes that smile away the tears. I have heard the measured voices lest a tiny crack reveal the impending sadness poised inside, all set to tumble out with the slightest provocation.

And as I stood with Phil at the top of the stairs, I wondered just how one really does find a way to stand where Phil stands—that dark place in life where all that once was, all the hopes and dreams and possibilities, seem so surely about to end, forever.

How does one go about the task of carrying on in the face of a partner's impending death? Where does one find some possibility, beyond the darkness, that is just around the corner? How does one truly accept the ugly fact that some dreams will never come true? How does one really reach the place where it can be said with acceptance, "What has been, is enough; what won't be, I can release?" How can Phil face life without his loved one and know their unlived dreams will never be?

I listened as he talked of his care for her and how her courage touched him so deeply. There is something profoundly intimate and sacred about life lived on the edge. Always the theologian, Phil continued, "I've been doing more thinking about hope. I'm not as sure anymore what it is, but I think it has something to do with accepting what is, and finding new possibilities in spite of it. Maybe it has to do with not expecting the reality that stares you in the face to change, though that would be so nice," and with that, he smiled a bittersweet smile. "Who knows? She's got a lot of determination and it may work out anyway."

Presently, a mutual friend of ours came by and the three of us walked down the stairs together, leaving for tomorrow the task of making sense out of this piece of life.

More Yesterdays to See
Than Tomorrows

I sat in my truck and watched Dad as he shut the garage door. His pace is slower these days and a recent bout with illness cost him some weight. Nevertheless, he's slowly pulling himself back together. He's had several of these spells lately, and I can tell that each time it gets harder to put his own health back in place. Mom has been sick, and that weighs on him and drains his energy as he tries to care for her, too.

I chuckled to myself as I remembered how he predictably talked about that night's banquet dinner: "Baked fish, new potatoes, and asparagus which, of course, I didn't eat," and other assorted food all correctly "blessed" by the Kansas Heart Association whose banquet he attended. That's Dad. Even in retirement, he keeps a full schedule and his own opinions.

Illness and the unspoken awareness that we all live in life's twilight these days brings us together in ways I had not anticipated. Once, I didn't think about what it would be like to see my parents slide inevitably and persistently into old age. It's painful to see those you love find life ever more difficult. And if I allow myself to see the truth of it all, I see my own decline as well.

Being young is such a joy. Youth is full of wonder and promise and unsoiled dreams. Sometimes I remember those days. Mostly, they've long since faded. Now there are more yesterdays to see than tomorrows. It's not that anything big has happened; it's more that the relentless passing of time takes its toll on all of us.

I looked at my sister standing in the darkness on the front porch with my mother and wondered who she was. I still remember her as my little blond kid sister. I never did tell her I loved her. We didn't do much of that kind of sharing when I was a kid. I'm not sure we really knew how. We missed something. Through the darkness, Dad slowly walked across the yard, stopped at the driveway's edge and turned to wave good-bye to me. In that tiny moment I glimpsed a window back to yesterday. His hair is white now and he stood with a slight stoop in the shadows. That's the way it is with age. Ever so slowly it settles all over and before you know it, it covers you. It seeps way down deep into your very soul until that's all you are— old. If it's not your bones, it's your spirit. They wear out and you get weary.

In those yesterdays, we never really learned how to enjoy each other. Dad always had work to do or bank examiners to worry about or a board meeting some place. We never learned how to talk to each other about the unimportant, everyday things which, if you really think about it, matter most of all. But I know the deepest truth, so I lay no blame. The sins of the father really are passed to the sons. I buried these same ordinary moments of life with my schedule, too. A whole wall full of certification papers and degrees remind me of where my time was spent.

He smiled as he waved good-bye. That happens more and more these days as first one brush with mortality, then another has startled him and he takes more time to smile. The close calls with tragedy have their place. More than ever, we know how we matter to one another. Aging brings fresh priorities.

As I sat in my truck I wished the impossible: that I could give my parents back their time. "If only" we could slip back to yesterday and craft the seasons all over again. Perhaps in some ways we spent a lifetime being with each other just as we were tonight: one of us in the shadows and the other ready to move on to some other place. It's hard to look at the twilight time and not feel some sadness.

But then again, as the evening shadows of life fall, the press of the day and the claims of life lessen and there is more time to reflect. Yesterday's mistakes really need to stay in yesterday. Sometimes I wonder about the fulfilled dreams that once brightened Dad's life, and also about the ones that died even before they were born. I wonder if he still hides dreams in secret, knowing they will never come true but which still bring a silent smile to his spirit when he is by himself. It's dark enough now to ask and there's still time enough to talk about what matters most of all.

Still, I'm beginning to understand and appreciate life's twilight. The shadows are softer. The colors are gentle and kind. Even darkness can be a friend; it's not all ghosts and goblins. It's an occasion to slow down and let the deepening shadows provide enough space to tell the stories. Evening is, indeed, a time to listen and remember the once-upon-a-time days. Those unimportant, everyday thoughts can still be spoken, and they still matter, most of all.

Trust Even When Fog Shrouds
Your Vision

Like the deepening of night itself, a thick gray winter fog steadily settled over the city, hiding everything it touched. Here and there swirls of fog drifted over the nearby construction site just outside the hospital window as the wind blew the mist like tumbling leaves in a winter wind. The fog was as relentless as illness. It persists and hounds one until, in its own time, it takes over and there is no way to avoid it. I strained to see the building project below, but I only saw blurred images of scaffold and steel girders nearly hidden in the deep gray vapor. The twelve-story giant yellow crane I remembered from yesterday was barely visible as it melted into the thickening clouds.

The stillness of the afternoon was interrupted when I heard someone say, "Oh no, Mrs. Sanchez, it's not night. It's only two in the afternoon, but the fog is so thick it seems later than it is." Across the hall the nurse talked to the hidden Mrs. Sanchez, who was taking her first-ever dialysis treatment. "Perhaps you'll get used to the treatment and it won't make you feel so queasy," the nurse reassured the unseen one. There are few secrets in a hospital. Sounds carry with uncanny clarity and even strangers know your tale.

Always in the background, the Muzak sounds of the season reminded us all that it was Christmas in the hospital. Inside my family's room, it was quiet. One by one the help arrived, each one dressed in the uniform of their role. Those in blue drew blood, those in white lab coats were physical therapists and they wondered, "Do you feel strong enough to walk yet? No? Then perhaps tomorrow." Nurses all wore stethoscopes and the physicians were set apart in their green scrubs and surgical shoes or designer suits.

A nursing student took vital signs, then recognized me and said, "Excuse me? Aren't you Dr. Shane? I thought so. I knew you from the nursing home in Newton when I worked there and you saw our residents. I want to take your Death and Dying class if I can work out my schedule." Somehow, it felt comforting to know that a stranger knew me and maybe would be especially attentive to my loved one. I guessed she would have as much to teach as to learn, though, and I was humbled to think that I tried to teach something as significant as death and dying to those whose very work exists in the shadows of this monumental occasion.

Christmas in the hospital. Outside in the city's malls, folks still shop for Christmas presents. Down the hall from this room, a tree stands, all dressed in ornaments and offering its pleasant air of festivity. The nurses wore brightly colored shirts in an attempt to lighten up the dreadful reality of illness.

But I find more comfort with the fog than with the season's costumes and customs. It sets a more authentic scene and speaks the truth that must be heard. Illness, like the fog itself, has settled over my family and overshadows the rest of life. Christmas seems different when it is lived at the brink. Here and there strangers walk past our door and their eyes tell the tale of choked-back dread and of anxiety held at bay. Eyes turn away from me at the elevator lest a stranger see the tears that fill my sleepless, weary eyes. People smile, though. We all smile through our sorrow as if to try to brighten the day of someone else and to deny the dreaded specter that haunts our own lives.

Hospitals are great levelers. Illness respects no one. Help comes from all quarters and I find a redemptive comfort in that. Black, Hispanic, Lebanese, Anglo, Asian: they all care for my father. Perhaps there is no more powerful a message that everyone matters than is found in the hospital where the everyday acts of care are offered by common folks to patients who suffer from illness and injury regardless of their background.

But it's the fog that summons me. I look so deeply into the winter mists that I see back to Christmases of long ago. Way back to the once-upon-a-time days when illness and disability were as yet undreamed-of horrors. Life was sweet, then. And fresh.

This time will pass. The magic of medicine has more wonder to give us and we will likely leave here wounded but wiser. And grateful. But changed just the same. This moment offers us the truth which is like the deep gray fog outside this window. Destiny stalks us all with a silent inevitability. It is not in our hiding that we find comfort; it is in our acceptance of community and in our willingness to trust in others even when the fog shrouds our vision.

I'm Still Walking Home with My Dad

"Tom, look at me!" said Dad from the far end of the hall. Hearing his voice, I turned in my chair and was delighted to see him unexpectedly walking toward me. Cautiously and somewhat unsteadily he slowly approached, always looking straight at me as if to make sure I saw his triumph. These were his first solo steps since last November. His face smiled with a joy I hadn't seen for months.

His thin hands grasped the silver walker for support and step by step he approached the couch and then, with the nurse's help, he turned to sit beside me. Like a crack in time, this moment caused me to remember my childhood with him even as I remember so many first-time triumphs of my own children who also said to me with a similar ecstasy in their voices, "Daddy, look at me!"

The relentless process of aging has brought me to this lonely reflection and now I follow a destiny as old as humanity itself. I stand between the generations and am parent to my adult children as well as my own mother and father. I scarcely know how to do either very well. There is no preparation for such a task.

I looked at Dad sitting beside me, still keen of mind but thin and frail in a way I've never seen him before, and for awhile I reminisced. It seemed only yesterday that Dad's words were mine and I was the unsure one, reaching out to be noticed and undergirded by him.

"Daddy, look at me!" I would say.

I didn't think this day would ever come. I am bewildered by how quickly the years have vanished. It seems only yesterday that I stood on the sidewalk waiting for the bus to drop him off a block away and I ran to meet him and we walked home together. We didn't play much ball nor did we go camping, but we walked home together each night and that activity itself, as well as what it symbolized, held its own value for us. If you can go home together, it makes up for games you didn't play or the fishing you didn't do. But you have to have a home and you have to know the way.

Life took a turn last fall and I don't think we will ever walk this way again.

The move from home to a retirement village when health fails is such a mixed blessing. If it offers increased security, it causes the loss of the comfort of one's own space. A home is not left without a lot of grief. I know that now. Home for my parents is now a clean and proper retirement community. It's not the place with the family room and the cozy fireplace they built. The new place is home in name only. It seems unlikely they will ever live together again in the old homestead and be content to live there in memory.

It wasn't so long ago that my sister and her husband and Linda, my wife, and I wrapped our parent's household treasures in newspapers and placed them in boxes for moving. Before then, I had never given much thought about what it feels like to touch someone else's treasures. A lot of memories are collected in fifty-two years of marriage. Each crystal bird or box of old snapshots recalled a story. Each old drawer was filled with memories: some good, some sad. We all laughed as we wrapped their items, trying to make light of this life-changing episode, knowing all the while that we were really trying to dull the jagged edge of this unwanted change.

It was Mom's idea for our daughter Kim to move into their place and it seemed wise. We cannot lose too much at any one time or we could lose heart, too. It softens the transition somehow to know that the home is still in the family and that a grandchild now lives there.

Soon, when Dad was all worn out by the activity, I stopped my reminiscing and laid him back down on the couch. There's less energy these days to do the necessary things that once were easy. What used to be so ordinary now takes an intentional, calculated effort. These days he lives between diminished health and destiny. In some ways I am still walking home with him. It's lonelier than I thought it would be, but there is a quiet comfort in the journey together. And sooner than I want it to be, it will be my turn to walk home, too.

A Splendid Teacher
for a Difficult Lesson

"How did your doctor's appointment go?" I asked Mom.

"Well, not so good. I'm disappointed. The doctor said I couldn't have the treatment. My tumor is not the right kind, so it won't work."

For a second it seemed as if the whole world was quiet. I was stunned. I heard her words and was surprised, both by the harsh reality they conveyed and by the sadness I felt building inside me. I had expected her to find one more exotic procedure which would give her yet another remission. All of us had put so much hope in the new procedure which we assumed would work more magic. But it seems not to be so. Reality is stronger than wishful thinking.

For fourteen years and three surgeries Mom has found some way to triumph. But life and luck both have limits. I didn't want to believe that there would be no more treatment procedures and that we were soon to face this final episode. But that seems to be the truth.

It was the melancholy edge and the sound of her voice that saddened me as much as the words themselves. I know of no one who has more inner strength to face life's adversity than she has. Always before there has been some distant possibility—some untapped resource—which she could find, then nurture into another chance.

Regardless of the crisis she has always found a way to beat the odds. Without thinking so, I just assumed it would happen again. I knew she was trying to find this faithful reservoir of her strength to rest on just now, but what I heard was a silent sorrow waiting to be born.

The days since this latest news have been wearisome. It seems only yesterday that Dad's health faded day by day and I kept the adult child's vigil, watching a parent I love and respect relentlessly fade into a broken and frail body unable to care for himself and needing help with ordinary human functions. Perhaps nothing is so tramatic as to see yourself decline until strangers must help with even the most basic personal needs. It is difficult for parents and families alike.

In the middle of Dad's vigil, Mom had her third surgery for brain tumor. I stayed with Dad in Wichita. My sister accompanied Mom to San Francisco for surgery. I suppose without awareness, I have wanted this respite to linger without limits. And surely I wanted to avoid having to endure yet another vigil with another parent, needing to be present in the difficult task of slowly saying good-bye as a loved one fades by inches. How naive I am.

For now, life seems to continue as it always has. Her relative health and independence hold steady in a fragile way. But I close my eyes to the reality I see gradually unfolding. All of life yields to the force of illness and decay. Nothing that is precious is ours forever.

And so I stand at the turn of yet another of life's corners. Soon enough this relative stability will crumble and I will know darkness. I have barely found my way after Dad's death, and now it seems another crisis is building, much like a prairie storm which mounts on the horizon then rushes upon us with a consuming fury. It is no small task to grieve. I have been there before. It seems much like returning to a place I once knew but have long forgotten, only to recognize it as it comes to me again.

It may well be that the magic of medicine will hold off destiny. But I know the truth. Remission is different from recovery. Each day offers me an occasion to express one more truth that I never found a way to express before. Each day gives us time to make amends . . . to celebrate memories . . . to have a cup of coffee and to tell a story. Each day is an opportunity to try to understand more fully who this woman is who gave me life and whose history makes me the man I am.

"She said I would have headaches and get more confused," said Mom. Then she added with a hopeful twist, "But I might not see any change for maybe two years." I wondered to myself, "Is that a long time or a short time?"

The truth is, I hate this part of the journey. I hate to see a parent live with the knowledge that all that gives meaning is relentlessly slipping away. I hate to watch her work so hard to be the person she has always been. I detest the obvious signs of her failure—the confusion. The overwhelming loneliness that engulfs her days. The life lived more in memory of what was than any vibrant joy in what is, because so little exists anymore.

But I treasure the good fortune of knowing that the courage I see in her everyday life will continue in my memory until the day when I will need to recall how she met her dark days with grace and dignity. She is a splendid teacher, but the lesson is so hard to learn.

Pieces of Pineapple

She sat in the chair, slumping uncomfortably on her right side. The evening meal was on the tray a full arm's length away. With the persistence that has been her lifetime's trademark, Mom steadily ate at her supper. I watched her effort. Pieces of pineapple tumbled from her spoon onto her nightgown. Her left hand lay limply in her lap. The left side of her face drooped, making her features appear oddly out of shape.

"Do you want some help?" I asked. "Huh-uh," she said passively as she continued to feed herself. More pineapple littered her lap. Believing that her nutrition was more important than her self-reliance, I decided to intervene anyway.

As I did so, I found myself angry at it all. As with most of life's concerns, the really significant events are experienced in ordinary ways. Had I not happened into her room just then, she would have bravely continued to feed herself with an admirable persistence, but with inadequate results.

She should have been sitting straight up. The tray should have been placed within easy reach, and not so far away that it was a strain for her to eat. An aide should have helped her to eat so that she got a full meal and not just pieces of it. Health care, once a standard of excellence in our culture, has declined. The paradigm has shifted. In our urgency to re-engineer our institutions to make them economically viable and profitable, we are paying the price in human compassion.

I watched Mom as she sat in her chair. The ravages of the brain tumor are increasingly evident. In the past months the signs have become dangerously apparent: multiple falls, slurred speech, poor judgment, difficulty swallowing, difficulty standing, little left side movement a passive acceptance of it all.

And so we wait.

It is not easy to be present when a loved one inevitably drifts from vitality to dependency. With each moment I must decide whether to take over some of her functions in the interest of her safety and well-being or whether to hold back, hoping that she will hang on to her diminishing abilities for independent living and a free spirit for as long as possible.

There may be no more important human quality than dignity. When illness robs us of this, we lose something fundamental to our being. It forces us into a morass of unwanted dependency on others. If we are lucky, those who attend to us will love us. If not, we will be left in the care of strangers and fate.

Those of us who care for our frail elderly parents find ourselves dealing with the dreadful decisions about their living arrangements, their medical choices, and their financial matters. We try to make wise decisions even as we remain emotionally faithful to our dear ones who have less and less capacity to understand what is being done to them.

My sister and I still pay the emotional price for taking away Mom's car over Thanksgiving. We probably allowed that privilege of driving to continue longer than was wise, anyway. To intrude on another's right to self-reliance is an awesome responsibility. When we make the judgment that someone we love can no longer function with the same independence they have always known, and we take away their car or we explore options for a retirement facility, we turn a corner from which there is no return. If it is right that we do so, so is it right that we appreciate the cost of our care in our decisions.

Somewhere in California a surgeon examines an MRI and compares this reading with his surgery on Mom four years ago. A stranger holds the fate of her medical decision in his professional judgment. Will another surgery promise another respite? Will it slow the ticking of her lifetime clock? Will this be the time when we will face the truth: all that it is possible to do has been done?

I go home at night and watch my grandson as Sara feeds him. One grandson. One great-grandmother. They are so far apart in age and circumstance and yet each is closer to the other than they can know. And neither one can understand or will remember this time.

But I will, for at night I sit in the silence of my home and think of how close we all are to one another, even though we do not understand it. All too soon it will be my turn. I am not sure we can prepare for such a time unless at some time in our lives we have to feed a loved one pieces of pineapple.

Holding Hands Until the End

I watched as the old man held his wife's hand. He caressed it tenderly with the familiarity of one who has held that hand for half a century. Though he talked with me, always he gazed sadly but affectionately into her face. When her eyes were opened they seemed to stare blankly past him as if seeing another world. Her unresponsiveness didn't matter to him. He was as attentive to her as if she could respond to his every touch, word, or gesture. It seemed less his duty and more his commitment. In a culture which values people for what they do or have, I found myself in the company of two people who knew the art of presence.

"There's not much hope now," the husband said matter-of-factly. "The doctor said it was a massive stroke and it's just a matter of time." He grew quiet as he put words to this awful reality. Saying something this momentous takes courage. "They tried to take her off the breathing machine yesterday. She tried so hard to breathe on her own but she couldn't."

As he spoke, his voice cracked and he turned aside. Some truth hurts down deep in your soul and this was one of those times. To hear another frame this reality in words is to hear the secrets of the soul; one must hear with kindness and respect. It is a burden to hear such a story. It costs. "Were you with her at the time?" I asked, wondering if he saw her desperate struggle or if he was just told about it.

"Oh, yes!" he said, wanting me to know this for certain. "I stood right here. I held her hand the whole time. We've been married fifty years, you know. I couldn't leave her, especially not in one of the worst times. It wouldn't have been right. She would have been there for me."

A smile crossed his face as he thought of their mutual commitment to one another. For better or for worse and for a lifetime, too.

I thought of how hard it must have been for him to have held her hand and watched while she gasped for air. He must have wondered if their fifty-year journey together was going to end before his very eyes. But no matter how painful it was for him to have to watch, there was no question of his being there. It was unthinkable to leave. And in the depth of her agony, she felt his gnarled old hands which have held hers for a lifetime.

I stood beside two old people who live life from inside yesterday's values. Their commitment didn't seem quaint or odd. It seemed more like a treasure that is too seldom prized today.

Today we talked of ordinary things around which priceless memories are crafted. "We used to have an icebox," he said. "I mean a real icebox . . . the kind where squares of ice were cut from the lake then put in boxes to cool things. There was a pan underneath to catch the water but Dad was a plumber and built a copper tube to let the water drain away into the sewer. And when Ethel and I got married, we bought a real refrigerator. Not an icebox, mind you, but a refrigerator. We bought it in '46 and it still works today!" He smiled as he told this story. Not so many old refrigerators or old marriages last this long. Some do, and they tell of a time long past when life and values were different.

Sometime soon this marriage odyssey will end. All too quickly my white-haired friend will walk silently away from this beside and say his final good-bye. His heart will hurt in ways most folks will never know. He will know a silence deeper than most ever experience.

Oh, but he will remember: iceboxes, horse-drawn milk trucks, their first Chevy, then the new Mercury. And though it will change nothing, he will find some comfort in knowing that even in the worst times, he held her hand to the very last.

PART II:
AT THE MOMENT

When my grandmother was terminally ill, someone from the family took turns being with her in the hospital. I don't know who made that decision or what their expectations were. The stroke my grandmother suffered was so devastating that there was no expectation of recovery. We were there to wait with her in her room and offer presence. She was unconscious and unresponsive, so we could only sit while she labored to breathe. Most of my extended family members seemed comfortable with this, but not me. I was terrified.

I knew she was dying and while I had no *experience* with such a human event and not any understanding about what would happen, the whole process seemed unnerving to me. I don't recall what I *feared* it would be like, other than it seemed terrifying to be with someone who would be alive one moment but dead the next. In those days, my cousin worked in a hospital and seemed accustomed to working with the sick, so it did not seem to bother him. I wondered how he did it.

Once, I took a turn to wait by her side. So long as Grandma's labored breathing was rhythmically predictable, I did all right. But one time it stopped for awhile, then with gasp and a groan, she began to breathe again. Terrified, I jumped up and felt overwhelmed with fear. I don't know what I was afraid of. Somehow, it seemed threatening to know she was at the edge of life and that my grandmother would soon cease to be. If fate had its way, it seemed likely that I might witness the actual moment of her death.

But it was not to be. She lingered past my watch and my cousin took his turn. I excused myself and went to work, relieved to have missed the awesome event when one life slips into eternity. It is indeed an unparalled experience to be present at another's death.

I was able to be present when my youngest child was born, and I cherish this hallowed memory. To witness a birth is exhilarating. I was filled with awe and wonder. I wanted to hold our baby and feel her new life touch mine. I wanted to hold my wife, too, and let her know how much I loved her. I felt as if I stood on sacred ground, and indeed, I believe I did.

The transition at birth from existence in the womb to a screaming, breathing human being is wondrous. It is a time filled with joy and hope. Life seems fresh and unspoiled and full of sweet promises.

But not so when the transition is from life to eternity. Even when a religious faith gives promise of an everlasting life there is, nevertheless, a melancholy ache which pervades the event because we are saying good-bye, not hello. And good-byes hurt.

Even so, the moment is marked with wonder and, just as birth, can be a time of comparable awe and need not be terrifying.

If I was terrified to stand watch at my maternal grandmother's deathbed, I was at a different point in my life at my mother's death.

Mother's breathing was labored and she seemed to gasp for air. I looked at her face and remembered my lifetime with her. The old pictures on the dresser told the tale. Beautiful, with slight build and an enchanting smile, she must have turned a lot of eyes. There was a picture of Mom and Dad standing together with Mom nearly full term with me. They looked at each other with fondness. How quickly fifty-four years have melted away.

I sat in a chair at the foot of her bed and watched her. Her breathing sometimes stopped, then started again, just like grandmother's. Apnea is very unsettling to experience and to witness. With each cessation of her breathing, I thought death had finally snuffed out her life. But then, out of nowhere, she would breathe again. Then stop once more only to breathe again. And so went the cycle.

Sometimes Mom's eyes were open and I would stand close, hoping to make contact with her through the haze of her unconsciousness. The times when we could talk were long since past. What I hoped for was that in this final episode, seeing me and hearing my voice might bring her some comfort.

I understood better why my family wanted someone to be with Grandma. Though it changed nothing, it at least meant that she would not be alone and those who loved her would be with her and bid her farewell. Maybe it was only important to me. Maybe the time when our presence could make a difference to her had long since past. I'll never really know.

Joe, the aide, and Craig, the nurse, stood silently nearby. They never said a word and I appreciated their silence. I didn't want conversation or comfort. I wanted to sit in the quietness of this place and let yesterday's memories tumble about me in odd ways.

I recalled when I finished my Doctor of Divinity degree and had some thought of law school; she encouraged me. "Do it while you are young enough," she said and added, "You can do it if you want to." I always knew Mom believed in any dream I had . . . even ones beyond common sense.

Sensing that Mom's death was imminent, Joe and Craig gently excused themselves, leaving my sister, her husband, and my wife and I alone with Mom. Then as silently as a thought, there were no more breaths. Not a one. We waited for a long while to see if she would find one more breath to grasp, but it was over.

I was relieved. No more did she struggle to breathe. No more would her mental confusion bewilder her. No more would her never fully recovered total knee surgery hurt. Old childhood beliefs emerged from the shadows of my life: now Mom and Dad are together again and once again they can look into each other's eyes with affection and comfort. Their three-year loneliness without each other would be over, and Mom could be with all her family members who preceded her in death.

How I hoped that all those beliefs were true and not just a Sunday School fantasy.

My sister, who had been seated on a chair next to her husband, came over to me, sat on the floor, and held my hand. I don't remember the last time when we gave each other comfort. In the silence of this moment, I had to face the truth that it is easier for me to give care than to receive it and it is easier to give care to strangers than to care for my own family. And it is hardest of all to let others care for me.

If I felt relief that her suffering was over, I questioned if I had given her adequate care. Did I see to it that she had enough pain medication? I think so, but wonder. Her mouth must have been as parched as sun-baked concrete with her mouth open wide, gasping for air. I never swabbed her lips once, hoping that the nurses did, because I could not.

But I was there. Even when it was past the time when she could willingly interact with me and when I even wondered if she could comprehend what I said, I would talk with her just in case she might understand. I told her I loved her. I told her that she was a good mom. I told her that I knew it was a hard time. I told her what seemed right to say.

She never responded. Her face was passive as if broken by a stroke. Brain tumors leave much the same devastation. Her eyes looked past me as if I were not there. But sometimes, tears filled her eyes and slipped down her cheeks and fell to the pillow. Sometimes tears say it best, anyway. To be present at the moment of death, is to stand in the presence of the Holy.

The stories that follow are the vignettes of some who have stood so near the point where life meets death. Perhaps in their tales, you will remember a time in your own life when once upon a time you, too, stood on Holy Ground and watched while someone dear "crossed over," a term which once seemed so quaint and odd but which now seems so true.

When Life and Death Hover Together

"Level I. GSW to head. Code Blue. ETA 10 min." The coded, cryptic message took seconds to cross my pager screen but promised a lifetime of sorrow to the strangers I would soon meet. A Level I trauma was on its way to the Emergency Department and would arrive in ten minutes. It was a gunshot wound to the head. I shuddered as I imagined the horror of the event. Not far away in an approaching ambulance a stranger hovered between this life and destiny and was being brought into my life.

Ten minutes was all I had to brace myself for the anguish I was soon to encounter. Time enough to speculate about the event. A suicide, perhaps? A hunting accident? A violent assault from a robbery? Perhaps a gang shooting. Maybe it made no difference at all what it was; it was enough to acknowledge that it had occurred and was coming Code 3 to our Emergency Department and I would be a witness and a participant in the event.

I signed in at the Trauma Room and waited. Surgeons in green scrubs arrived. So did x-ray technicians and respiratory therapists. And nurses, too. I felt reassured when I saw one of the surgeons whom I had seen work before. I liked his self-assured calmness. Security officers stood outside the Trauma Room; it was a gang shooting after all.

A jumble of conflicting feelings pulled at me. Emergency work is mystifyingly exciting. It is an arena where a team of keen minds still their emotions and jump with supreme confidence into the midst of trauma to push back the forces of chaos so that life and hope have another chance. I stand in awe at their willingness to touch the raw nerve ends of life and faith. They work as much by calling as by training and because of their conviction as much as for the salary they make.

But I always stand alone in the Trauma Room. It is mostly a place for technicians, not storytellers, and I know my place. If I watch in admiration I am haunted by the horror of what I see. Too often, deeper than the frenzy of the care in the Trauma Room, what I hear is the shattering of the dreams of parents for their wayward children who have become lost in the thicket of drugs and gangs and their tragic need for revenge. What I see are young people who have walked down dead-end streets and who are then brought into my life to die right before me.

What I hear loudest of all is the absolute stillness of unnecessary death and the weeping of parents whose hearts are forever broken. Too often I see sturdy bodies waste away to skinny frames which never walk again because a bullet shattered a spine.

All too soon, Unknown John arrived. His clothing was cut from his body and he was prepared for the magic of modern medicine with its tubes and machines and procedures. As I watched them work over him, he seemed so still.

I don't have much stomach to watch trauma work, although I have learned to detach myself enough to observe the process. My calling is not to procedures of cure so much as to the art of care.

Too quickly for my comfort, bits and pieces of family arrive, having heard rumors that a family member was shot. "Is my son all right?" begs the mother who trembles before me and who continues to speak without waiting for an answer. "Oh, dear God, let him be all right. Oh, please, dear God!"

Standing in the corner of the room are two brothers who glare icily about the room and never smile nor weep. My own heart skips a beat as I absorb what seems to be their endless rage. I cannot imagine the anguish that has settled over their lives just now. I hope they will not seek retribution.

A hush settles over the room as the surgeon comes in, introduces himself and then says with a deft measure of concern and reality, "I'm sorry. We did all we could but he was too badly injured."

As if joined in common voice, which in truth they were, Unknown John's mother and little sister grab each other and scream in horror. Their worst fear has come true. This beloved son and brother has died too soon, too violently, and too unnecessarily.

The streets have taken one more life. I am as angry as I am sad that we have lost our way and some of our youth. My heart cries with the parents with whom I feel a kinship that transcends color or nationality lines or income or educational levels. When your child dies so needlessly it hurts as deep down in your soul as you can ever hide. I fear we have lost our way and there will be more broken hearts. Way too many more.

Children Are to Be Loved, Not Hit

His tall, thin frame stood silhouetted against the white X-ray screen which revealed the skeletal images of a tiny child. Seeing me beside him the doctor asked, "Tom, how did the funeral go?" referring to a recent funeral I did for a child who died as a result of child abuse. I told him what I thought.

"That was our third child in a month," he said, with a note of mournful disdain to his voice. "I don't know how we can get the message to adults that you can't hit your kids! Period! No matter how stressed you are, you can't hit your kids! They'll die!" With that he turned to walk out the the unit to attend to more sick kids.

Still young himself, already he has seen more sorrow than most people. After all, a person like this in a place like the Pediatric Intensive Care Unit sees the most severe cases and it is so clear how cruel life can be. It's enough to break your heart every day.

I have only been in the Pediatric Intensive Care Unit since January, but already the unit is crowded with mournful memories. Sometimes when it is quiet I can still hear the anguished father's bittersweet and crackling voice sing the soft sounds of a lullaby as his child lay so silent and still in the crib. "Hush, little baby, don't you cry. Daddy's going to sing you a lullaby. . . ."

Only the sounds of the infant's ventilator whispered the truth: the child was only alive because the magic of machines kept him so. And once the grandparent from far away arrived, even that magic would be removed and then the truth of it all would be known and the child would slip from this life into eternity.

I wondered how barren was the heart of this young father who may have been the very one who bore responsibility for this catastrophic loss of life and innocence. In a moment of rageful frenzy one adult lost control and his fury cost the life of his own child, the integrity of his marriage, and his own innocence. The joy and hope of his heart is now filled with shame, regret, and utter remorse. But it changed nothing.

There is no lament or anguish strong enough to turn back the clock and undo such fury. All the tears, all the years, all the remorse, are all too little and too late to undo the sorrow.

And if I work here the rest of my life I will not be able to erase the bitter sorrow of watching another young mother hold her tiny months-old baby in her arms waiting for nature to complete the course so tragically started when a boyfriend, baby-sitting for the evening and with not enough experience or patience to know how to respond to the crying infant, shook him until he experienced a massive brain injury.

I watched this infant grow ever more quiet and unresponsive in his mother's arms. The sacred space where the mother, her family, the nurse, and I all stood our vigil was shrouded with a cold silence: at long last the child had died and was at peace. I wanted it to be otherwise. We all did. But no yearning on our part, or in our hearts, changed the awful truth that child abuse had claimed another innocent life. I swallowed the lump in my throat, dried my eyes, and left the unit.

When a child is born, we are reminded of how life begins in innocence and with great hope. Unable to do anything but exist, babies teach us patience as they constantly demand our attention. Without our love and affection they will not thrive. In our very hands exists the destiny of a tiny sacred life, waiting day by day, even hour by hour, for our nurturing love and care.

Sometimes I notice that a deep silence settles over the PICU, a silence louder than all the crying of babies or the bleeping of machines. It is the silence of all the children who would tell us, if only they could, to find another way. The silence is deafening. It surely begs to be heard. Children are to be loved, not hit.

When Tomorrow Comes Too Soon

I sipped my coffee and listened while Joan talked about her work. Her enthusiasm for her work with autistic children and their families was evident. Her dark hair hung about her shoulders and I watched while men stole second looks at my attractive cousin. We did the usual updating of family history so that each of us would know the current stories of our families.

"I had a few free days and my workload isn't heavy yet so I decided to come back to see your parents and Aunt Velma, and Aunt Mildred, too." She paused for a moment as if trying to find a way to talk about the obvious truth: this may be the last occasion to visit some of them. Age and frailty have robbed the older ones of our family of their health and clarity of thought. Deep shadows are falling over their lives and promise a forthcoming silence.

Sometimes their memories are only as long as a day and they must make monumental decisions even as their capacities for understanding seem to slip father away from them and they don't know it. Joan has made this journey before when first her father and then her mother died a few years ago.

I nodded in agreement and let her know how important it was to all of us that she came. If we all once lived in Wichita, our separate journeys have cast my cousins across the land. "I'm not sure Mom ever forgave me for moving to California," chuckled Joan. As she did so, I was caught off guard at the familiar sound of her laughter. As if by magic I heard her mother, my Aunt Jaye, once more. A flood of memories washed over me and I could see my aunt's presence in my cousin's face and voice. Instantaneously they developed for an instant, then melted, never to be touched again. And I was sad. Had I known how fragile are these moments, I might have opened myself up to them and held onto them longer. I was too young to know that then.

Joan understands the redemptive power of presence. She understands that nothing lasts and that it is worth the effort to reach out and hold a moment before it slips forever into yesterday. Joan understands that perhaps our memories are the most important of all our creations. Intangible as they are, they nevertheless have the power to sustain us when life is difficult and give us hope when life seems empty. And if we are lucky, these memories can be shared with those whom we love for they, too, can "remember when" with us. For a while last week, Joan and I reminisced about old memories and crafted new ones for tomorrow.

"You were so good to Mom before she died, " Joan said to me. Her eyes momentarily glistened with remembered grief. "You understood when she failed and wasn't as clear as she once was."

For a while I remembered my own visit to Fort Collins just three years ago. I was on the other side, then. Once I knelt by Aunt Jaye's recliner while we talked about the olden days and she expressed her hopes about what I would say at her funeral. Now it's Joan's turn to witness the vigil and to be present while her cousins wait.

Joan waits as one who understands, thought and not as one who has only "hearsay knowledge." She waits as one who understands how ponderous are some decisions, how relentless is the undertow of failing health, and how lonely it feels to know that tomorrow has come too soon, and fate is quickly making you the oldest one.

Whatever unfolds in the time to come, for one evening, someone touched my life and reaffirmed my belief that life is best when lived in community.

The Loss That Has No Equal

One by one they arrived and took their places. A half dozen scrapbooks lay on the mahogany table with decades-old photos inside which told the story of their lives with an unmistakable and unyielding truth: these were old friends in every sense of the word. The once youthful, fresh faces of the albums are now lined with deep creases. Most of their hair and beards have grown snow white.

The clear bright eyes of youth have given away to the reflective eyes of wisdom and the experience of aging. What once seemed to be an eager look of hopeful anticipation in the old pictures had settled into the weathered look of life review to those who sat around the table. Life and experience do that to a person. With time and experience we look back more than we look forward. There are more yesterdays than tomorrows to see. And, oh, what stories we all have to tell.

But beyond the rust of years, this group has long ago learned that life must be lived in community. For only within the context of love and support are the inevitable burdens of life made endurable. Slowly the chatter subsided and Jerry said, "Charles, I want to hear what you have to say. We all came to hear your story."

I watched as Charles reached for one of the shiny red apples from the silver tray. With his pocket knife, he carefully cut it into slivers to eat. His cuts were careful and precise. Graciously, he thanked Ray for the courtesy of the apples as he said, "I can't eat the spicy stuff anymore like I used to. This is nice." He smiled as he spoke. It grew quiet in the room as the crisp apple snapped first with the cut from his knife and then when he took a bite. We waited in silence until he was ready.

It was hard to be here and we all knew it. We were here because of our love and respect for one another, but mostly we had come together to hear the story . . . Charles and Frances' story . . . of the agony of saying their final good-bye to their dying daughter. If some things are only ours alone to endure, there is, nevertheless, some redemptive value in knowing that others will be with us in spirit and support as we face our destiny. And so it was that we met in Kansas City to share the burden of old friends who just now knew the dark night of the soul.

With his own health failing and seven decades of life weighing upon his breaking heart, and with his devastating grief of his daughter's recent death to contend with, he looked frail . . . almost broken. Even so, Charles sat with the grace and poise I have always known him to have. His lifelong partner, Frances, sat by his side. Tears spilled unashamedly down her red cheeks as her husband told their story.

There is no harder task for parents than to give up their child to death. Such a moment knows no equal. It can rob your very heart and soul of vibrancy, leaving you dazed and barren. Such a loss is out of rhythm to our life expectations. How bitter to watch, helplessly, while a treasured child fades and fails and the ravages of illness or an injury steal hopes and dreams as they tumble too early and too certainly into the abyss of death. Left alone, and broken in spirit, parents feel a void too deep for words and almost too dark for hope.

"I told her it should be the other way. She should be saying goodbye to me. I'm old and I've had a good life. She's young and has two daughters . . ." and his voice trailed off in memory as the searing pain of losing his adult child once more throbbed in his heart. Frances buried her face in her hands and she sat passively while another friend caressed her shoulder and whispered softly, "I'm so sorry."

Life is filled with loss. All kinds. Things. Health. Places. People. Hopes. Dreams. But no loss is worse than the death of your child. Such a thing can break your spirit. But if you sit in a circle with old, dear friends who have themselves spent time in the wilderness of loss and know that landscape, who know where the really barren places are, and where there are places to rest and people to succor you, and who have arms big enough to hold you, and hearts willing enough to listen to your sorrow, then such a desperate and frenzied time can at least be eased.

When I left that day, nothing had changed and no one expected it to. The grief still throbbed. The loss still seemed inordinately jagged. But Charles and Frances told their story to a community who listened because they were loved. And we all listened knowing that one day it will be our time to sit in this community and feel the support we all so surely need. To tell your story and be understood by friends is in itself healing.

Death Strips Away the Veneer

The four adult males towered over the tiny casket as they wheeled it into the sanctuary. Somehow it seems to me that caskets should be big—the size to fit adults—for then it suggests that a big person has died—not a child. When the casket is small enough to carry in your arms, there is no denying the mournful truth that a little one has died. The death of a child seems savagely mournful to me.

I sat by myself in the sanctuary and looked across the way to my hospital colleagues. They sat together as if to console one another. A friend's baby had died and we had come to the funeral for the last farewell. We sat in silence, alone with our thoughts. Though most in the congregation were strangers to one another, we nevertheless seemed to find community in our shared tears and silent weeping.

I remembered how just a few weeks ago the grieving mother held her child while she visited with us in the unit. Seeing me, the baby smiled as if I were a familiar friend. I touched his arm to acknowledge his greeting. He seemed to purr like a contented kitten. Looking at his smiling mom I teasingly remarked, "He could come home with me for a visit if you would let him."

She smiled at me. Acknowledging my playful remark to her child the mother remarked with a wistful look about her, "Nah. We're staying close together these days. He's going to Denver for surgery in a couple of weeks."

For a moment it was quiet around the desk. Mom caressed her baby and he smiled in return. The other nurses looked away in sadness to guard their own grief for their friend. I felt unexpectedly lonely.

However much all who loved this family prayed and yearned for the miracle of restoration, it was not to be; this wee one died. And so it was that we gathered at St. Vincent De Paul Roman Catholic Church to share our tears and hear the words of hope and comfort each of us needed for our own private reasons.

As the tenor sweetly sang "Jesus Loves the Little Children" I looked about the sanctuary. Not far away I saw a physician who is used to seeing the violence of the Emergency Department. I wondered if he is touched by the suffering he sees. He seems so professional and remote from it all.

But not today. He put his arms around his wife and held her close. She reached for his hand and squeezed it. He seemed lost in love and loneliness all at once. I found a comfort in seeing his warmth and compassion. Death does that to us. It strips away our veneer leaving us with what matters most: our need for comfort from our loved ones, known through their warm embrace and their kiss of our tearstained cheeks.

Near me sat a group of paramedics and sheriffs' deputies all in crisply pressed blue shirts and shiny black boots. Long since used to seeing life's ugliness, they also sat in stoic silence. Still, their very presence seemed to say something of the respect they held for this broken and aching young couple.

When you teach a course on death and dying and work as a hospital chaplain and conduct funeral services yourself, as I do, you develop a certain professional protection. But as I sat alone in the sanctuary I sat not as a theologian or educator but as a lonely man who remembered my own losses and the times I buried my own grief so that I could be available to help someone else.

On this day I sat as one who needed to hear words of hope and comfort. I needed someone to tell me that in the debris of broken dreams and so much pain, the Good News still matters.

It also helped to be at St. Vincent De Paul. The last time I was here, it was nothing but a pile of ruins, all blown to pieces by the Andover tornado. But today, the green carpet and creamy white walls and cathedral-like ceiling spoke silently of renewal after destruction. Hearing the splendor of the piano and the voice of the tenor fill the hallowed halls with rich wonder reassured me that there is hope after chaos.

Grief takes a long time—probably a lifetime–to heal, if it ever does. But it helps if you do so in the context of people who, in their own way, have known sorrow and who hear your grief as a familiar song which they know all too well. Grief summons us together to care for one another.

The gentle voice of compassion spoken by the priest was also healing. Though nothing was changed, it seemed easier to bear. When I left, I saw the midday sun and I felt the prairie wind caress my face and my tears were dried.

With the Gentleness of the Setting Sun

I watched while the old one stood by his wife's bed. He caressed her hair, then kissed her on the cheek. His hands trembled and he sobbed a single, mournful lament, then stepped back. Dressed in blue jeans, denim shirt, and black field boots, he looked like the farmer he was. His face was tan and tough and he squinted from years of shielding his eyes from the sun.

A daughter caressed her mother's leg, then dabbed her eyes with a fresh tissue. One by one the entire gathered family gently touched the dying woman and bid her farewell. Not a word was spoken but each kindly touch seemed to carry a lifetime of memories. Groans too deep for words and touches which conveyed truths that words could not frame became the source of comfort for this family—that and the redemptive silence which let each one remember the days gone by.

With her eyes open the old one stared vacantly past her family into a deep and silent void. I wondered what she saw.

It is hard to die. It is hard to let go of the everyday perceptions that make you who you are: the sound of your daughter's voice, the way your husband touches your face in a caress that you've known for fifty-four years. The familiar creaking of your own home wherein you loved and raised your children.

In the twinkling of an eye there comes a moment when it is time to let go and trust that the hope and faith that you've proclaimed has taken root in your soul and will carry you into eternity. But no one lets go of all that is loved without a struggle. All too soon we stand at the edge of life and wait to hear our name called.

The magic of medicine was over. The tubes were gone. It was time to stand in silence and wait in the company of one another and let a lifetime of memories tumble from the forgotten past and bless this vigil.

Probably none of us standing around the bed truly understood the reality of the monitor screen's symbols but we knew enough to realize that as the squiggles smoothed to several single, solid straight lines this loved one had melted from life as we know it into eternity. The nurse ever so slowly reset the monitor on the wall with each beeping sound so that it, too, faded into silence. And then it was finished. It seemed so ordinary. So subtle. So quiet. With the gentleness of the setting sun the old one died.

With the compassion of one who, in her own time and circumstance, has waited this vigil on the other side, the nurse touched each family member as they left the room. Her own eyes were wet with grief and she took a tissue from the box I gave her and wiped away her own tears.

I never quite get used to it, this moment of final farewell. I wanted to take my shoes off, for I seemed to hear a voice from long ago telling me that the ground on which I was standing was holy. It seemed to be.

The respiratory therapist had disconnected the breathing apparatus. The RN had adjusted the monitor. The priest whom I summoned had anointed the patient. The MD had pronounced her dead. And me? I was present. I was a witness. I listened. I remembered. I touched. In some strange way I saw my father again, as he relentlessly faded from life to death in another room much like this one. I remembered how it was for me, then, when I stood in this family's shoes.

And I thought of my students and how difficult it is for them to stand in this place. I remember how frightened I was at Presbyterian Medical Center in 1969 in my first summer's clinical training unit when a young woman—younger, even, than me—told us she was dying and I knew I was inside a feeling I had never experienced before and I was not sure I could stay there. I wanted to flee and find my friends and family and be reminded that life can be joyous and sweet. But I stayed and learned something about how to be present in these times. What I gained in knowledge I lost in innocence. A single instance of pastoral care with one family in one tiny room in a setting filled with technology and it all comes to a moment of redemptive presence.

I am about the task of helping students learn how to stand in silence and listen to the sound of tears as they spill from a husband's eyes. I try to help students learn how to be quiet and not rush to proclaim a truth, however wise it is, because just now folks need to remember and they need to cling to each other. I seek to help students learn to watch the faces of nurses who, themselves, do the messy work of healing then see their patient die anyway. I help students learn to hear the voice in the burning bush tell them to take off their shoes, for the ground on which they stand is sacred. I hope to help students listen to the silence of their own lives and see if they find any Holy Presence there.

A Season Out of Time

When I arrived at the scene of a Christmas Eve house fire, black smoke was already pouring from the windows. Inside, I could see the orange flames darting about underneath the thick smoke. Sometimes the blazing flames jumped through the windows. Mostly, they seemed to stay within the house as if to devour every living being and every solid thing within.

"There's kids in there, Tom," said one firefighter to me. "We've had men in with Scott packs on since we got here, but we had to get them out. They ain't got a chance and it's Christmas Eve." One by one, the walls grew black from the searing flames. The howling prairie wind made it miserable to work outside, and fanned the fire into a frenzy.

But nothing lasts forever. Not even the agony of the Oak Street fire. In due time, the flames were extinguished and there was nothing left but white steam which rose from the ashes of the house. A firefighter took his helmet off for a moment and steam rose from his perspiring head, making him look as if he had a halo.

"Found 'em." came a cry from inside. "All of 'em," an unknown firefighter responded matter-of-factly.

I never get used to it, this business of trying to bring a measure of healing and comfort to families suddenly thrust into hell itself. With a police officer, I went to the hospital where the three bodies were taken. Two surviving siblings and the baby-sitter who had awakened from naps and escaped the inferno were safely there, treated put on the for minor injuries and massive fright. And Mom would be there as soon as she returned home. Christmas shopping in a nearby city, she left the children with a baby-sitter who also took a nap when the children all went down. How could she know that one child would awaken, play with a cigarette lighter near the tree, only to see it explode into flames and engulf the house?

"Thanks for coming," said the hospital chaplain. "We've got three code yellows and two code whites. We're waiting for Mom to return home to tell her."

The chaplain's presented words were professional but cold as we all were. You have to be professional to work with such horror and you must hide behind your presenting coldness. How else can you wait for a mother to come home to discover there is nothing left of her house but a blackened hollow shell of charred ruins? You have to find some way inside yourself to brace against the inevitable agony you will experience when you tell the young mother that three of her babies burned to death.

Three, I said it. They didn't just "die" or "pass on." They *burned up* when one child, playing with a cigarette lighter, caught the dry Christmas tree on fire and it mushroomed into a billowing, raging inferno which seemed to explode like dry prairie grass in a drought.

The hospital chaplain was professional, all right, just like the physicians and nurses and cops and firefighters and EMTs. There is no place for amateurs and curiosity seekers in such circumstances. Only those who can stomach the agony of utter horror need be there.

But as I looked about the emergency room, I watched as the rest of the staff behaved just as I did. I kept to myself and didn't want to talk. I kept thinking about everyday things . . . like how I had to call my friend, fresh in town from Cincinnati and tell him I couldn't meet him because of this horrible event. Little things like how the teller at my bank turned ashen-faced as my pager went off and she heard my side of the telephone conversation with the dispatcher. She exclaimed, "Oh, Jesus, I hope no one's dead! Another customer said he drove by and saw the whole house boiling in flames. Just before Christmas!"

There in the ER, we all hid behind the mask of doing our jobs, but inside, I guessed they felt the same churning in their stomach as I felt. The silence was broken when the police chief said to me, "Tom, I need you to return to the scene. The mother just arrived." Another matter-of-fact message that spoke the truth: Go to the scene and be with the parent. I dreaded that, but it was the *deeper* truth I feared most of all.

Usually, it's that way; the truth *deeper* than truth burns the most. I was to go back to the heart of the event, the still smoldering, burned-out shell where at that very moment a young mother surely stood in disbelief. Her burned-up home where once life was fresh with laughter and kids' puzzles and baby toys, was now a black hole of destruction. Absolutely nothing could make it right. There are no words of comfort wise enough to make hope seem real. My destiny was to be present in the dead center of chaos and hear the wailing of this parent who would see the truth and hear the words, but not want to believe what she knew to be true.

I stepped out of the officer's car and nearly slipped on the thick buildup of ice that covered the street. The subzero winter wind added its own misery. Everywhere it was cold. Frozen spray frosted the north side of trees. Black-helmeted firefighters in thick black boots crunched over the crusty ground where water from the hoses froze as it hit the air.

Strange how quiet it was. Right there in the midst of hell itself it was quiet. "Why is that?" you say. Because the firefighters had just given their absolute best and it was not good enough. And that hurt. Firefighters went about their tasks in stoic silence, knowing they had worked by the book, yet feeling in their hearts the bitter realization that their best was still not enough. The silence set the tone for their own private questioning of the meaning of it all—if indeed one can find even a measure of meaning in what seemed a senseless tragedy.

"Tom, they're in the neighbor's house," said an officer, when I arrived. I approached the small frame house next door and though I was still outside with the north wind raging, the empty moans of a grieving mother could be heard as she sat on a couch, cradled in the arms of her neighbors. "Oh, my babies. My babies. It cannot be so! I want my babies back!"

There is no sadness to match the unyielding grief of a parent who discovers her children died a terrible death in a season out of time. There is never enough comfort to give a parent to ease the anguish of such consuming despair. Trusting the instincts of the human soul, those closest to her sat nearby, held her, and wept.

Sometimes the only response that counts is to be willing to sit in silence and absorb the tears of the grief-stricken survivors. Make no mistake about it, there is no more blessed call, nor harder task than that of *doing nothing* but being present. In such times, one wants to run away to someplace where children smile, where others laugh, where someone accepts you with a warm embrace because for that instant, life is sweet with splendor. But sometimes such moments can't be found and the only place to be is where another sits on a couch and buries her head in your arms and weeps. The hot, bitter tears will stain your soul and you will forever be marked because you have accepted the grief-born anguish of another.

Sometimes I get lost inside my own memories as I try to make sense of such times. When we were back at the hospital with the mother, I remembered each of my own children, now mostly grown to adulthood. In the mother's wailing I heard the enduring love for her children and how desperately she would have given her own life for their safety and future. In her grief, I tasted my own remembered tears of joy at how breathtaking was the joy of each of my own children's births. In those days each of my children's lives seemed fresh and untouched by sorrow. Possibility smiled at each one. I remembered all those silly games I played with them: made-up games which no other family ever played because they were uniquely ours. And I remembered how each of my children and I, in turn, would sit in their darkened bedrooms at night before sleep and together we melted into the magic world of fairy tales as I shared tale upon tale with them. Stories no one else ever heard because they were born out of my imagination and in response each child's wide-eyed wonder and giggle. They were *our* stories.

As I fought back my own tears, I wondered how this family could survive the destruction of their own dreams and memories. I wanted to hold my children and save them from such horror. I wished desperately that this family had their children to hold and love. But for now? It was enough to lay aside my own remembrances and be present in another's endless, unyielding despair.

"Janet," said the hospital chaplain. "Janet, we'll take you into the room where your children are. This will not be easy, Janet. You must understand that before you go in and see them, that your children died in a fire, and that will make it hard to witness. They will not look the same as you remembered them, Janet."

Inside of me, my own heart thundered. Part of me wanted out. I wanted to run. I didn't want to see the truth I knew lay so still just inside the door. I was glad the other chaplain had to name the reality. I wondered how she found the grace to speak such horror with such tenderness.

Things seemed to be going too fast. I wanted to slow down the whole tragedy so I could have time to brace myself. But tragedy has a pull all its own, and as if swept by a silent current, we entered the quiet examining room and there gave witness to the truth that grief work, when children die, has no equal.

As if by fate, or the grace of God, the family's priest was present for other reasons and when I saw him, I asked him to be with us. Together we stood side by side in the small examining room and watched as the chaplain unwrapped the tiny children for the mother to see.

Oh, how I wanted to heal that moment. How could a parent look upon her own children so still, so small, so wounded and ever face life again? How could she believe that in some unknown day, she will ever know peace inside herself again? No trauma is so evil that it breaks the bond of love and beyond the anguish of what she saw, the mother cradled her babies and wept.

"Why, Father, why? Why?" begged the young mother to her priest. Why indeed? There are no answers that satisfy. There is only the observation that into the midst of such barrenness, other decent folks chose to be present. Neighbors cared. Churches gathered goods. Friends knew enough to swallow their advice and simply hold these broken folks and cry with them.

It was quiet that night at the fire station. Here and there firefighters stayed to themselves. A few talked together and tried to console one another. As if to name the truth and thereby prove it real, one said to me, "Tom, when we rolled up the whole structure was engulfed. Flames were already leaping out all the windows on two sides. We did our best. We did. It just wasn't enough." With that he looked away to shield his own tears while adding, "They're my kids' age, Tom. I thought of my own kids and when I went in there, I couldn't find them. Too much heat. Too much flame. Too much debris. I just couldn't find them. But I tried, Tom. I really did," and with that, he hung his head and wept.

Some wounds never fully heal. Oh, they get better and we go on. We learn to bear up and cope. But we never forget how once upon a time we peeked into hell itself.

I hear her weeping still. I always will.

Stan Smith's Brother

"Tom, this is Debra at Dispatch. We've had a suicide and we need you to respond to seven-oh-one-oh South Random Road. It's Stan Smith's brother."

I heard her words but didn't want to believe them.

"Stan Smith's brother?" I asked, hoping I had not heard her correctly.

"I'm afraid so. Stan Smith, our deputy."

My heart was heavy. Stan is a friend. He's a deputy. He's solid and you can count on him. We joke around a lot and he can brighten the day with a light touch.

"His sister-in-law found him and called Stan on his cellular. When he got there, he confirmed it. He's there now, Tom."

"I'll be enroute right away," I said.

If the dispatcher's words were businesslike and to the point, the underlying message was heavy with sorrow. One of our own was drawn inescapably into an abyss not of his making and from which he could not run. His brother lay forever still because he chose to take his own life. Survivors of suicide pay a lifetime cost. Oh, they survive and even put their lives back together in time. But it leaves their spirit broken for a long while.

I drove quickly along the country road to the small town. I felt a great conflict in my heart. The next day my wife and I would be leaving for a long-awaited vacation. A dream trip, really, and I was awash in eager anticipation. Our son surprised us with an unexpected visit from Texas on his way through town and I cherished the expectation of an evening visiting with him.

But it is inherent in law enforcement that tragedy sets its own pace and respects no one. So I tried to set aside my own concerns and issues because just now a good and decent family and a friend had plummeted into a tragedy and needed all of our support.

And in my heart I could not ignore the truth that, this time, the sorrow was to a law enforcement family and that alone made a difference to me. And was it really only last night that all of us were called out to work a drowning? So much grief in only twenty-four hours. But this time, the sorrow was within a law enforcement family.

Already the house was cordoned off with bright yellow "Crime scene. Do not cross" tape. Until the final disposition was clear, the tragedy had to be respected as a potential crime.

Stan stood alone on the gray concrete front porch. He reached into his breast pocket and pulled out another cigarette and lit it. Through the blue haze of the smoke, he looked past the nearby hedgerow, staring vacantly into space. No matter how many sorrowful events you have worked as an officer, the moment is just as raw, and hurts just as deeply as it does for anyone else, when the tragedy is personally yours to experience and not simply and incident to work.

"I'm sorry, Stan. Dispatch called me and told me. I came as soon as I could." I put my hand on his shoulder and was quiet. Sometimes a compassionate touch conveys more than words. It's hard to hear, anyway, when you hurt so deeply. Stan shook his head to acknowledge my presence and concern.

I walked inside the small frame house with the investigating officer. For reasons I do not fully understand, it helps my work when I witness the events that the officers, paramedics, and family members have to see. Only then do I more fully grasp the weight of what they have experienced. Even so, my work is always removed from the emotional intensity that they must experience. Still, being there and seeing it seems to help my understanding of my pastoral work.

In the far back bedroom, Officer 918 quietly took measurements of the room. Another deputy looked carefully at the items in the room and took pictures. Officer 904 and I stood silently together in the doorway.

On the floor just beside me lay Stan's brother. I tried to imagine how overwhelming it must have been when his wife first discovered him and how unfair it was for Stan to have to see his brother in such a tragic circumstance. It was so quiet in the room I could almost hear 918's pen mark the measurements on his notepad.

I looked at Stan's brother and felt a great sadness. I wondered what had turned so sour for him that taking his own life seemed his only option. I wonder if he ever had even a wild guess of what devastation his ultimate decision would wreak on his several brothers, his wife, and his parents. I wondered what secrets turned in his heart with such fury that he lost all hope and needed some desperate and sudden release from his pain which was so silent but so severe that he saw only one option: to take his life.

Officer 918 continued to measure the scene while another officer looked for a suicide note and took pictures. I stood beside the forever still body of this beloved man, who got lost in misery and saw only a final, tragic exit, and I contemplated what weary thoughts he had in the few minutes just prior to his fateful decision.

However much we yearn for answers, sometimes we must be content to live with unsolved mysteries. It helps to have colleagues who care for us and who can be present without words. Cops are mostly "fix it" people. Problem solvers. Action-oriented "doers." We feel better when we put the pieces back together again. But often as not, our work puts us in touch with the painful truth that some problems can't be solved. They can only be accepted and lived with. Like suicide and a friend's grief.

Sandwiched Between Sorrow and Joy

Dad opened his eyes and looked toward me but he didn't seem to focus very clearly. He looked beyond me as if I were transparent. I greeted him, hoping that the sound of my voice would help him collect his thoughts and rally. But some moments are too hard to bear. Some realities are too hard to face. Although awake, he seemed lost in another world. Sleep seemed more appealing than the Medical Intensive Care Unit (MICU) with its tubes and procedures. I could hardly blame him. I wondered what he thought about, shut off into himself as he was. It was a world I could not enter. I hoped he found comfort in remembering his once-upon-a-time days when his life was still unfolding and filled with the sweetness of fresh dreams.

Life is so much richer when you look forward with great expectations to your dreams than it is to lay still, broken in body, waiting for the final number of your days to come to pass. It is painful to realize that there are very few, if any, dreams yet to see. How quickly it all melts away. Memories die slowly, and reality is hard to face. Sometimes the only comfort we know is the final release from suffering, but that blessing is difficult to accept. There is no coming back from that relief.

Overhead the monitor displayed its scientific truths about heart rate, respirations, and blood pressure. The green jagged lines were relentless in their story. I could look right at them and never understand that his inevitable slide into death was imminent.

Outside his room, the nurses' station buzzed with hospital chatter. Down the hall, a TV telecast the Kansas-Colorado basketball game. Only a wall and a hall separated life lived vibrantly from life lived at the brink. It is easier to be a chaplain who gives comfort to others than to be an adult son who stands on the receiving side of care.

It seems strange how suffering often holds within it episodes of redemptive joy which temper the pain of illness. My nephew and niece flew in from Texas. They are adults now, but I see childhood memories crafted into their adult lives. I am glad for my memories of those times. They are reservoirs of comfort when life seems barren. I like them as adults as much as I did when they were infants.

It is bittersweet to see one life fade even as you see others in love with their hopes and dreams. That cycle is as old as life itself. And some of us were sandwiched right between them both. Sorrow and celebration. Bitter and sweet. Hello and good-bye. Life lived in between.

"I took your Dad in to see about his driver's license just last week," Mom said. I told her at the time it was an empty dream because of his fragile health. The cataracts on his eyes caused his vision to be hazy at best and he'd never pass the vision test. Anyway, he could not walk. I had hoped to spare him one more loss. But they tried anyway. It was all a desperate hope that these losses would melt away and life would be fresh and hopeful once again.

"They were so kind to us," Mom said. "They gave him an identification card and a three-month extension. I didn't even know that was possible. That made him feel like a human being again. He may never drive again, but this helped." It is the most ordinary things, often done by strangers, which help us feel so human. Like an extension of a due date. And being treated with respect. It's hard to feel much dignity when you are worrying about dying.

Not everyone takes the time to do his or her work with compassion. But somewhere, an unknown official saw that the gift of dignity offered in kindness made that last ragged edge of life easier to bear. It brightened the life of a frail old man who will never drive again, but who was respected and treated decently anyway. How quickly even that week-old gift fades.

We've been here before. There may even be another respite. But one day there will be no return. One day the vigil will be over and we'll say our last good-bye. For now, it's enough to sit for awhile as the machines relentlessly tell the tale and we wait in silence.

Finding Hope in the Midst of Suffering

It was the big elm in the front yard of the first home I ever lived in that I wanted to see today. I remember it well. At about shoulder height on an adult, the trunk split into three branches of equal size so that like a great armchair, you could sit between the branches and lean back. As a child, Dad would pick me up and sit me there when I asked him. I thought it was scary because it seemed so high. But Dad was there to lift me up and take me down.

As I drove by the house, I was startled as I looked sadly at the tree. A big red X marked the trunk and the branches were cut down. The tree was dead, trimmed to a stub and soon it, too, would be gone. But I have my memories. The truth is, I wanted it to be alive; but even trees, like life and memories, fade and fail over time.

The houses along the street seemed older and smaller. On the corner, Shannon's Market was boarded up and a rusted lock hung on the door. In its own worn down way, it told me that I cannot go back. Things have their time, but that time passes, life goes on, and you can never return again in the same way. Still, I needed to visit this street and browse among my memories.

My first five years were lived on this street and I learned fundamental lessons about life in this house. Grandma Shane had her stroke here and I first faced the mystery of major illness and death. I learned how family and friends come together, and how life is forever changed. I also learned how you can go on anyway and find fresh hope, though at the time it seems impossible. Memories are made from the everyday chunks of life as much as they are from the great events. This was an ordinary time and an ordinary street.

As I left the house and drove on to Mom's place, I remembered last night. At 2:08 a.m. the phone rang. The whole of last year had been preparation for this moment. "Tom," said my sister, "the hospital just called. Daddy died a few minutes ago." I wasn't surprised, though I was sad. It was expected and it was a release from his suffering. Linda, my wife, held me for a long time and we didn't say a thing. A tight knot stuck in my throat and tears filled my eyes. Grief is eased when you are loved. It won't change a thing, but the moment is redeemed and made easier to bear.

Life takes a twisted path and weaves itself through both the majestic and the mournful. And sometimes both come at once. For over a year, kidney failure resulting in dialysis, congestive heart failure, and diabetic complications had worn Dad down. Sometimes it seemed the slide would go on forever. But even suffering has an end.

As hard as the year was, it served a purpose. Beyond the routine of daily life and sometimes in spite of it, life brings new opportunities. A doer all his life, Dad rarely was still or reflective. Emotion was foreign and to be avoided. He talked about the practical things, but not much about the meaning of life.

Until, that is, there is no more ability to do anymore and there is nothing else to achieve. These are the times when one can only be. And being is best anyway. I regret every suffering moment of his last year, though the secret blessing is that it opened the two of us up to ways of being we had never known before. Sometimes I would shave him and we would talk. Never one to say "I love you," it became apparent that saying what was in his heart took on great meaning. And so we found out how to relate to each other and tell each other how we felt. You are never too old to need a blessing and it's never too late to give one. If you are really lucky, you and your parent can become friends.

By the time I got home after attending to some necessary arrangements, our kids were already arriving. They need to know how to experience this milestone. In the meantime, our own memories will silently come and one day, too, they will bring comfort.

When Tears Say What Words Cannot

Linda placed a bite of food to Mom's lips. Instinctively she opened her mouth to receive the sustenance, but that was all she could do. Whether she was too tired or had forgotten how, she didn't chew her food. "You need to chew your food, Mom," I said, hoping that my familiar voice might summon her from the wasteland of her unresponsive world.

It's difficult to know what does help her these days. This last indeterminate period of her life seems to linger on without mercy or relief and there are no familiar landmarks to guide our course. We wander, hoping that what we do and how we are brings her comfort, but we cannot be sure.

It is hard to die. The journey from life as we know it to our eternity is difficult and those on the path are so frail and weary that they find very little comfort on the way to the relief that death may bring. I watched in disbelief as the staff at the Village put thickener in Mom's water. I never knew that water could be so hard to swallow that it needs to be thickened.

Most of the time she lays in bed with her eyes closed. It's what we were told to expect. She will sleep longer and more deeply until she finally slips into a coma never to wake again. Knowing this gives us clues to watch for and makes each decline predictable.

Understanding what will happen next makes each waking moment precious because it may be the last one we ever share with her. But this kind of knowledge does not lighten the burden. It is hard to watch her fade bit by bit and see her struggle with every ordinary daily living task, like swallowing and breathing.

Sometimes Mom opens her eyes and looks about. To a casual observer it might seem as if she is at least passively taking in the world around her. But I know better. In these moments when her eyes are open I kneel beside her chair and try to engage her. I have learned to realize the truth that from somewhere deep inside her vacant eyes she stares past me and sees a world far beyond this one. A blank look covers her face. She lives somewhere deep inside her world of yesterday and waits for tomorrow. I am not sure she is even here, today.

We have passed the time when words are useful. They were yesterday's way to communicate. Once we thought that we stumbled onto a clue to make her life easier when we all talked about our ordinary routines, hoping that as we did so, she might feel included in our daily lives. For awhile it seemed to work. Then that, too, faded. We wonder if she attends to us at all these days.

Not so long ago when it was bitterly cold outside and the prairie winter matched the coldness of our hearts, I said to her as I left, "I love you, Mom." She turned her head on the pillow ever so slightly and mumbled in her slurred speech, "I love you, too." These were the last words I ever heard her speak.

Mom is here in body but is lost in another realm, or so it seems. But I have learned to attend to her essence, not just her presented self, and not give up my belief that because she doesn't speak, she doesn't comprehend.

Once I looked at her and it seemed to me as though her struggle was exhausting. I tried to name the truth as I saw it when I said, "This is a hard time for you, Mom. I'm sorry." She stared blankly beyond me, as if I were not there, but from her eyes, tears tolled down her cheeks. In some ways I believe that she does hear and tells us so with her tears. This is the time of life when tears tell truths that words cannot frame and when silence is shared because that is the only gift left to give.

I tried to wonder what it must be like to have a tumor in your brain, crowding out your life. I wonder if she is afraid or if she hurts. I wonder if her memories give her comfort. I wonder if our daily presence makes a difference to her. Does she know that each night Linda sits by her side and feeds her? Does she sense when our daughter, Sara, cleans her room every day at the Village?

Someday, both this time and her life will end and we will say our final good-bye. Until that time, our task is to wait and to offer presence.

PART III:
WHEN DEATH IS TRAUMATIC

Both my parent's died from natural causes. I always thought that was just a way to say that death wasn't done to someone in some catastrophic way. I suppose it was a way to ease the pain. It was a way to remind us that since death is inevitable, if it happens naturally—because we "wear out" or "catch" a disease—it is easier to bear.

There is some truth to this, of course. It *does* seem harder to accept death when it comes too soon or too violently or because someone else has viciously caused either one's own death or the death of another. There is grief either way, but when it is *caused* by someone else through intent or inattention, it somehow seems preventable and especially wicked. Following such a death, survivors seem to endlessly wonder "what if" something had been done differently or "how could someone be so wicked as to intentionally kill another." In such times, our grief is fueled by anger. If the traumatic death is due to a natural force such as a tornado, then we face the futility of our lives in the face of nature's impartial and relentless force.

If the death occurs because of some evil human act, survivors must reckon with their own bitterness and rage directed toward that other whom they believe to be responsible and whom they hold in contempt. Even those who find it in their heart to forgive, usually come to an understanding that forgiveness generally means a willingness to not seek vengeance—an intent to go on *as if* nothing happened—in full awareness that the absence of their loved one screams the deepest truth of all that something horrific has happened. Traumatic death is horrible for the one who dies and it leaves the survivors likewise ripped asunder.

Such events are as massive as the Murrah Federal Building bombing with its 168 causalities crushed, ripped, and burned to death in a single cowardly act of malice, or as isolated as a single suicide. They are as normal as the deaths that follow a tornado and as evil as a homicide.

Traumatic death is shattering. It comes too soon, it is too devastating, and it leaves scars that never fully heal. Whatever stability we thought we had is torn asunder. Nothing that was, is anymore. It is as if hope itself has died. It certainly feels to survivors as if they have died and yet they do not have the peace of death. They must go on with an aching heart and a sense of how cruel life can be.

Such moments are devastating for many reasons. The visual scene is terrifying for survivors as they must see the burned and lifeless bodies of their loved ones. Families of the Murrah Federal Building bombing disaster saw endless pictures of the shattered remains of the building. They had to wait while first hoping their loved one would be among those who were rescued then hoping that, at least, his or her body would be found intact or, finally that enough of a remnant could be found so that at least they would know for sure that death had come and they could have closure to this catastrophe.

Survivors are left with a sense of rage and anger that seems unrelenting yet with nowhere to direct their feelings. Sometimes, the cause is carelessness and the one who caused the agony meant no harm but now must live forever with the scar of knowing that he caused irreparable harm; like the child with the lighter on Oak Street.

Sometimes the perpetrator is unknown and remains forever lost in the sideroad of life. Then the survivors never really find closure. There is no justice, no answer, no redress. Survivors may spend the rest of their lives without the balm of closure. An emotional open wound will throb the rest of their days. They may learn to live around it or beyond it, but never with it.

Indeed, a piece of your heart and soul dies in the traumatic loss of your loved one. Gone forever is the laughter of your child or the comfort of your mother. Never again will you be able to ask Dad for a piece of advice because he was cruelly murdered in a blast from a stranger. The friend who knew your innermost secrets and whom you trusted with your soul is suddenly dead—unchangeably gone forever. You will live with a piece of your life never fully intact again.

There are some who know such a moment. In the twinkling of an eye, life was forever changed. Life will never be normal again. At best, survivors will have to create a new "normal," for the old one has passed away.

The stories that follow are the tales of a few who have known such a time. Listen to their stories with a sensitive ear, for somewhere they still feel the pain of a broken heart. For these people, death was traumatic.

Unleashing Memories from the Past

"Do you mind if I smoke?" asked the aging doctor. It struck me as a strange request. It was an act of courtesy, but it was offered in a time of chaos when such social graces are overlooked. Across the street, the barren Murrah Federal Building stood silently, a horrible symbol of death and destruction. We sat on the grass in front of the United Methodist Church with the green decontamination tent just behind us.

A pile of debris, bits of broken glass, and an assortment of other nondescript items lay nearby, swept into a huddle. The massive stone church structure itself was silent. Its windows were shattered. Sitting in the shadows of this, the oldest church in Oklahoma City, I had a sense that the building itself was sad. In a symbolic sort of way, I thought it was proper that the church was damaged. It was as if God had been in the dead center of the catastrophe and had been wounded, too.

But there it stood, silent, injured, but present. Empty of life, it was still giving shelter to those who sat outside as it served as a sanctuary for the dead who lay shattered inside. Somewhere deep inside this house of worship lay the ever-increasing number of bodies as they were retrieved from the Federal Building across the street and placed here for the time being. Like Joseph of Arimathea's tomb, if the building itself was ruined, its spirit, nevertheless, survived.

I was saddened that this church, a sanctuary for hope and Good News, was now a repository for those wickedly slain by an act of unspeakable horror and cowardice. And yet I found comfort that in some ways, finally, these unknown, unnamed souls and their families could find peace. For at last their fate was certain.

The doctor lit his Kool and inhaled deeply. The blue smoke swirled about his face and melted into the cold wind. Not far away a bulldozer scooped up tons of shattered bricks, glass, automobile parts, and dumped it into the waiting dumpster. Dust swirled about with each scoop.

"See that dust?" said the doctor. "It could be very dangerous." With that fact acknowledged, he explained in precise medical language the potential risk of inhaling the invisible agents of death that exist in decaying bodies and in other chemical particles found in such moments of madness within the debris itself. I watched the dust dance in the late afternoon sky and found myself covering my mouth as I breathed, hoping this would protect me.

"Wear this if you ever get near the dust," he told me as he handed me a mask. It was the same message I had heard an hour ago from a State Trooper standing guard at the fence. He, too, warned of the risks of contamination. There seemed no end to the horror of this tragedy. A silent specter of death hovered invisibly about us all and threatened even more evil to the helpers.

But the doctor didn't simply want to give me safety advice, though such a focus was an easy beginning point for his heart's real concern. It was his own personal story that he needed to tell. "My dad was a lawyer and everyone thought I would be one, too. But I had this passion for science and logic. Medicine is my only real passion. But before medical school, I enlisted in the Marines and I saw combat in Korea."

He paused as he inhaled deeply from his cigarette. His eyes looked intently at the massive pile of shattered debris at the base of the Federal Building, sometimes darting back and forth to the armed officers standing watch nearby. Sometimes he looked at me. But always he looked sad.

"I landed at a port city and right away I was in a battle. I killed a lot of people. But we were told to "suck it up" and go right on. So I did. No one helped me with the horror I saw or with what I did. No one ever has. And now this. I feel like I'm back in Korea in the middle of another battle.

"My wife divorced me some years ago," he continued, "and I was devastated. I cried for days. I didn't understand it. I went into therapy and my counselor said it was normal and that I was doing something healthy by grieving this way, this much. I thought my sadness was because of my divorce. I suppose it was. But I think it was for all the hell I saw in Korea, too, and never processed. Do you think so?"

Indeed. A time of anguish and horror seemed compressed and buried in his heart but never really processed. Never, that is, until this tragic event pulled him back to yesterday and his almost forgotten anguish. "I think a lot of these rescue workers will have bad memories to process like I've had if they don't get help."

As he talked I watched the rescue workers crawl across the pile of shattered and crushed concrete and steel not very far away from me. In single file they passed chunks of concrete and buckets of debris down a row of firefighters like so many ants working in line. I wonder what thoughts crossed their minds as one by one they removed chunks of wreckage hoping and dreading all at once that they might find a victim and bring to certain closure one more painful mystery.

Later, I stood by a mesmerized soldier at the recovery scene. "I found a shoe and a toy car," he said, matter-of-factly. No smile. No sadness. Just a blank account of his work. Stuff it down. Ignore the meaning that in your hands you held the shoe of a child who just might still be buried under tons of debris. Don't feel. Don't cry. Be the soldier that you are. And pay the great price that someday the memory will come back to haunt you and you will weep for the child who belongs to the shoe and who died in the blaze of hell itself or perhaps under a massive crush of concrete. Don't think. Don't feel. Just do your job.

I stood at the edge of hell itself when I worked the Murrah Federal Building disaster and I heard the groans of those who walked that way. A cold wind blew, but it came not so much from the north across the land but from the source of evil itself as it spread across my heart.

We have lost our innocence but not our decency. A few unleashed great horror, but many more offered love and compassion through their work of rescue and recovery. They dug through the carnage. They touched the wicked wounds of the injured. They listened. They cared for strangers. Hope lives in that rubble. It is just that it will take so long for it to blossom.

A Broken City

It's quiet in this corner of the command center. On any other day this would be a part of the lobby of the telephone company at 8th and Harvey in downtown Oklahoma City. I'm worn out and need time to myself to collect my thoughts and renew my spirit. I have listened to three days of horror stories and I need to find sanctuary in solitude.

Around the corner a group of MPs from an Oklahoma City military base doze on the floor. A group of Oklahoma City firefighters walk by. Their heavy yellow coats with bright yellow reflective tape squish as they walk. They leave a trail of water behind them as they pass by. Their dirt-smudged faces look exhausted. I wonder what they've seen in the silence of the great, vacant Murrah Federal Building a few blocks south. From this far away the building with its large gaping hole looks dark and forbidding. Rubble hangs by cables and large pieces of concrete blocks dangle precipitously from the walls.

I'm wet all over, too. Outside torrential downpour drenches this heartbroken city, and a cold north wind chills all our hearts, as well. It seems fitting that it is cold and dreary outside because that's the way it is inside each one of us who works here.

I spent the last hour walking about the disaster area trying to gain some sense or perspective of this tragedy. I need to do this. Something this devastating seems strangely remote until I walk through the broken glass and feel it crunch under foot. Then it stops being a story on CNN and becomes reality. But I hardly know where to start collecting my thoughts. This nightmare seems so big and monstrous that it is hard for me to organize my thinking.

I have been here since Wednesday when I received a call from my director who said, "The corporate office wants us to send people down to Presbyterian (a sister hospital) and help their staff. I'd like you and Carol to go since you are the leaders of our Critical

Incident Stress Debriefing Team." Because of this, I have spent the last three days listening to the anguish and anger of staff members at the hospital who worked with the victims of the bombing.

Though the staff members were not themselves hurt by the bombing, they are, nevertheless, victims in their own right. I can still hear their agonized tales of devastation.

"I was in the ICU working with my new heart (patient) when the whole building shook. I thought a plane crashed into the hospital," said one.

"I thought an elevator broke loose and crashed to the basement," said another.

"I thought it was some chemical explosion," said yet another. "The whole building shook. I held on to the desk at the nurses' station and then thought 'This is stupid, the whole floor will cave in.'"

On and on went the storie, some worse than others. A young male nurse put his hands to his face to hide his own suffering as if it were a point of shame, when in fact he was really showing us his human compassion as he said, "I'm too young for this. I'm only twenty-two. I thought I was just going to keep records in the triage room when they called me, but instead they sent me to the ER."

He shook his head in bitter anguish as if to cancel the memory of having to stand in hell itself.

"They brought in a victim and half his face was gone." And with this truth proclaimed for us to hear, he began to weep while a colleague held him in her arms and they both cried.

And so did I.

"They sent me down to the site with a box of tongue depressors," said another nurse in a hallway conversation.

"Tongue depressors? What do you need boxes of tongue depressors for?" she asked the man on the phone.

"So we can scrape up body parts if we need to," came the answer.

"I can't even touch one now," she said as she, too, cried in torment. "I'm not sure I can ever work again."

I walked by the chapel where a service was just beginning to offer comfort to mourners.

I can't say why, but when the music drifted around the corner to the hall where I was filming a spot for CNN, without warning my eyes filled with tears. They had been hiding there all along. What was it about the music that invited my tears? I will probably never know. I only know that I choose to be here because I believe I can offer a redemptive presence and because I can listen. But it comes at a cost.

The adrenaline flows like water. Everywhere I turn there are rescuers of some type. Yellow-coated firefighters. Rescue workers from San Diego. Heavy rescue workers from Phoenix. FBI, ATF, Secret Service, local law enforcement agencies. All of them seemed focused on rescue and recovery work and on doing the best job they can. Never in my life have I walked in such a center of energy.

I walk around with relative freedom because of my identification. I have a clear plastic badge with law enforcement markings because I am a police chaplain. Even so, I cannot go into some areas because of safety concerns. I've been told it might be possible for me to be escorted to the Murrah Building to give support to the rescue workers but that is uncertain. It seems the building becomes more fragile by the hour and the prospect of injury and disease grows as well. It may be that it will be quite awhile before I ever get in, if ever I do. But somewhere inside I see them walking around, those yellow-coated firefighters. Piece by piece they throw down the rubble. Piece by piece they uncover secrets. Relentlessly they work, hoping, yet dreading, that they will find some victim. Rarely have I known a situation in which pastoral care has been more readily received. It seems everybody is wounded and struggles to find hope.

The whole area is security conscious and armed officers stand at every corner demanding to see identification. It somehow helps me to see and touch the horror. It makes it real. To see this chaos on TV is overwhelming. To walk between the blown-out structures windows and see the many small neighboring buildings also smashed into endless bits of debris is to truly understand the depth of the devastation. There are a great many chaplains but only a few are trained law enforcement chaplains. In times of crisis, trust goes deepest when you are known as "one of them."

And so I wait. I wait for the removal of the children. I want to see if I will be called to help and to listen to the anger and agony of those who must, bit by bit, piece by piece, person by person, remove the broken promise of life in each dead child. There, I said it. Dead children. That's what hurts so much—all the dead children. A priest told me an hour ago that he was allowed on site when the first children were brought forth so that he could offer them a blessing. Every day one priest and one pastor wait at the morgue to provide sacramental care and pastoral presence.

"It was the least I could do . . . offer a final blessing to these children. It helped, although I know it changed nothing," said the sad priest.

But he was right. Even in their final moment, though they were unknown and unnamed, they were blessed by a compassionate priest who gave what he could: his willingness to be there and to touch their broken bodies and to give them the promise of salvation. That's all any of us can do now. Give what we can. Listen to the stories. Listen to those who cry. Be present. Pray. And weep.

How Are You? What Was It Like?

No matter where I stood, the haunting cavern of the Murrah Federal Building loomed over me like melancholy mist. Deep, dark, and dead, this building was still able to cast a presence over all who worked within its empty frame.

For a long while I stood at the chain-link fence on the west side of the catastrophe and watched as rescue workers carefully dug through the debris. This position is just in front of the post office, also severely damaged by the blast but nevertheless converted into an on-site staging center where hot food, sturdy clothing, and supplies were given to the workers. A local pizza restaurant made hundreds of fresh pizzas for everyone. Hot food to warm cold hearts.

At the command center several trucks were being unloaded and material was being distributed to teams of rescue workers who were supplied with the sobering tools of this trade. They were given heavy boots to wade through the sharp and jagged debris so they wouln't be hurt and heavy gloves designed to withstand their constant ripping and tugging at chunks of concrete, exposed iron bars, and shredded glass. And most unsettling of all, they were issued specially designed masks equipped to filter the air they breathed to remove the tiny particles of debris which would inflict fatal damage to the rescuers now turned to body retrievers and investigators.

The trooper with the large brown German shepherd standing guard by the equipment told the truth—the untold truth never spoken but known to all who work such ghastly events. "I got warm clothes and a jar of Vicks. It's been a week and as soon as it turns warm the stench will be unbearable. I've already put Vicks in each nostril to mask the smell and I'm not even in the building."

The whistle blew and the elevator on the crane removed a hundred or more firefighters. I stood near the gate and watched them leave. Some smiled. Some stared vacantly past the debris and the crowd of support personnel.

"How you doing?" I would ask.

"Me? Just great. I just do my job like I'm trained. It ain't so bad."

Perhaps. Staying focused helps. Not finding bodies helps, too. After awhile I learned to watch their eyes, for they told the deepest truth of all.

"How are you?" I would ask the ones with deep-set, empty eyes. They seemed to be the ones who saw the most difficult scenes and perhaps worked the most gruesome aspects of the tragedy.

"Can you tell me what it was like?" I would ask.

"I saw nine bodies, all crushed under the big concrete beam. It'll take heavy equipment to lift it off before we can retrieve them. We spent all day trying to uncover a file cabinet which was crushed under debris. We saw a pool of blood underneath it and it seemed likely there were bodies there, too, but we couldn't get to them."

I wonder how these nameless workers, which destiny has thrust into the deep secrets of this tragedy and who worked closest of all to its bitterness, will process this tragedy in the days to come. What visions and memories have been hidden inside their hearts which will one day have to be touched again. Perhaps in a far off time and place some new event will open the door to their "room called remember" and once again they will face the horror of this work all over again.

The rest of us watch from afar. We are touched by the tragedy. But these workers live inside it. They touch the dead and shattered victims so that they might be redeemed with dignity and their remains treated with respect. These are the ones who smell death. If it is a philosophical, evil tragedy to us, it is a dirty, stinking, fearful, and ominous event for the workers. And many of them were younger than my children.

As a cold wind blew down my neck and the brooding clouds spit cold pellets of rain on my face I thought of many things. This was one city. One bomb. One event. But one major catastrophe for us. It deserves all our mourning and every tear we shed. It deserves our anger. We have been violated and the security we thought so certain has been seen for the illusion that it is.

If we let ourselves swallow the whole truth, we must acknowledge that all around our shrinking world this much and more happens with evil consistency to others who are also innocent and undeserving of the tragedy that has befallen them. While this truth does not diminish the magnitude of our Oklahoma City nightmare, it sets our event into perspective and we must acknowledge that others, too, are ravaged by the forces of evil. Perhaps we will see how clearly we are all a part of the fabric of humanity and how evil crosses lines of color, geography, politics, and every other way we separate ourselves.

We are all more united in our grief and sorrow than we are ever divided by our political or religious beliefs. Sorrow knows no race or geography. It only knows the taste of tears and the empty wailing of parents who will never hear their infants again and whose arms ache in desperate yearning to hold their child just one more time.

Returning to the Scene of an Evil Act

The two vacant lots upon which once sat hundreds of media vehicles were empty. What had once been the site where the nation's news media camped and waited for scraps of information about the federal building bombing disaster was now a barren, silent, empty space. Across the street, the great stone telephone building where six months ago so much of the rescue effort support services were centered was now used for its intended purpose, serving simply as a telephone company.

In the parking garage, emergency vehicles had given way to ordinary cars. This was where we ate our meals, and received wet weather gear and medical supplies. It now seemed strangely quiet. The focused energy and passion so clearly evident six months ago was nowhere to be experienced. The massive build-up of law enforcement personnel and rescue workers had left. It all seemed strangely, sadly quiet.

I parked two blocks away on this, my return after six months to this place where once the nation's eyes were riveted as we all watched the painstakingly slow process of rescue work turn to the sad task of retrieval at the Murrah Federal Building. Though three of us from the hospital made this pilgrimage, I could not enjoy the company of my colleagues. I drew ever deeper into myself as we walked along the familiar streets toward the bomb site itself.

In almost every way, this fine city has returned to normal, or so it seems at a casual glance. The horrid destruction of six months ago has been cleaned up. Traffic moves up and down the streets where once armed guards stood their watch and kept a wary vigil on all who passed by. The debris of shattered glass and building blocks has been removed and I walked along the sidewalks without having to walk over and around the tragic chaos. Where I once walked on shards of glass and stepped over the broken pieces of building debris, I now walked on clean streets. Nothing crunched underfoot.

But no amount of effort could hide the scars, regardless of the efficiency of those who cleaned up the city. They are everywhere and each one silently screams the unrelenting truth: once something evil happened here. I walked by the old post office, now closed and guarded by a chain-link fence and faced the void where the proud Murrah Federal Building once stood. In its place there is nothing but an empty lot, now covered with sod. I stood in the same spot where six months ago I looked at the shattered, bleeding building within which folks worked with care and compassion as they searched for the remains of victims who were murdered in an instant of madness.

But no freshly sodded green grass hides the images which lurk all abut like invisible ghosts. I still see a nine-story building ripped apart by an evil act. I still see rescue workers crawling over debris, poking, prodding, and searching for bodies. I still feel the north wind rip through the urban canyon and drive the cold April rain down my neck. I peered through the security fence around the vacant lot and returned to yesterday. Deeper than the bright blue October sky above, and beyond the efforts to bless this spot with kindness, I heard the groans of all those whose lives ended in a millisecond. And I was sad.

I looked across the street where an old newspaper building sits with its roof ripped asunder and where large beams covered dark and empty spaces. Not far from the lot where the Murrah Building once stood, the United Methodist Church keeps a silent vigil. Quiet and empty, it is now only a relic. Once, faith was celebrated and pro-claimed here, but now it stands as a solemn testimony that evil does indeed leave a stain which cannot be overlooked. Although horror does not triumph, it leaves a scar on our cities and our hearts.

A chain-link fence surrounds the whole compound. Woven within the fence is an endless collage of memories left by well-wishers. Flowers, toys, T-shirts with messages inscribed, shoes, letters; all sorts of treasures mark the fence.

But no mark is greater than the awesome silence of this sacred ground. There is nothing here but memories. I stood in reverence at the emptiness. Those who walked by were quiet, too, as if they were in a holy shrine, which, perhaps they were after all. But it was less the sorrow of the empty buildings which lay open and exposed that troubled me and more the reality that this place is littered with broken dreams. Everywhere I walked, I sensed the anguish of all those who once had hope here, and now must begin again.

Between Chaos and Coffee

The nighttime breeze was raw. The rain had stopped but the damp wind sent a shiver down my back. Behind me in the ditch the paramedics finished packaging and then loading first the father, then the son.

The bright lights from the generator illuminated the edge of the field where the torn and twisted car lay on its back. The front windshield was shattered. A half-empty bottle of Wild Turkey lay oddly on its side inside the car. I waved my flashlight with the bright yellow cone back and forth and stopped the northbound traffic while the ambulance left the field, crossed a culvert, then turned north toward the city hospital. It ran Code 3 so I hoped there was good news. Maybe they were still alive.

As the traffic cleared, I stood in the thick darkness and watched as the officers took measurements and drew diagrams. A quarter of a mile away another deputy held traffic at his end of the scene. Together we let a single lane go north and then south. But for long periods of time, it was quiet on the cold spring night on the lonely highway. The nearby fields were pungent with wet soil. Overhead, the clouds were breaking up and a few stars peeked through. The storm was over, but the cold lingered.

As I stood by myself on that wet roadway, I remembered how the other officer had tried to joke with me at the start of our shift, "We are going to have an injury accident. I just know it. It's been raining and the public's forgotten how to drive on slick highways. You wait. It'll happen."

It seemed a cruel twist of fate that not five minutes later we were running Code 3 to a report from the dispatcher of a "single car roll-over, possible pins, two times." How quickly things change.

Presently an approaching car slowed to stop as it came near to me. In the inner darkness of the small car, I heard a panic-stricken young woman plead with me, "Oh, please! Are they all right? I think it's my husband and son. A neighbor drove by and said she thinks it's our car! Are they all right?"

I never get used to this—the desperate yearning of a loved ones hoping for all they're worth that their deepest, most horrid fear is not true . . . that it is only a mistake . . . and that this tragedy really belongs to some other decent family, but not to them.

I could only tell her the truth, that I did not know the condition of the patients but that they were taken to the hospital. Inside I felt a sense of relief come over me. If I couldn't give her the reassurance that both were well, neither did I have to present the wicked truth that her two greatest loves were forever dead or seriously injured.

Law enforcement in general and police chaplaincy in particular are peculiar pursuits. The camaraderie we have is rewarding and the excitement is fun. If such a thing is in your blood, it's just what you do. But the cost is high. Inevitably, we work at the raw edge of life where in the twinkling of an eye, families are shattered and lives are lost or completely changed.

I rode silently with the deputy as we approached the Emergency Department. It's where I work for a living, so I am known there. A few staff members did a double-take, seeing me in the blue jacket with "Sheriff" written on the back in big bright yellow letters. Either by jacket or profession, I was acknowledged and the deputy and I found our way in to gather data.

Inside the trauma room, I noticed that it was too quiet and there was too little activity. A few nurses attended to a few details but the reality was all too clear to me. There were no survivors.

Down the hall by the glass doors, I saw that the young mother had arrived and was pacing anxiously in the hallway. She watched every passerby and her ears perked up at each sound as she waited frantically for some word of hope, however vague and illusive it might be, that her loved ones were going to be all right.

"That the wife and mother?" a young physician asked me as he nodded toward the woman. The deputy and I both nodded in agreement. The doctor simply shook his head back and forth and then said to us, "Neither one made it. They were dead at the scene. It seems so damn useless. Dad was probably drunk and neither one had on a seat belt. They'd be alive if they would have. I feel sorriest for the kid. He doesn't deserve this." After saying this, he left the treatment room and walked down the corridor and stood beside the trembling young woman.

I was glad it was another chaplain's duty that night. Someone else was there to be attentive to this woman who was now, herself, a victim of the trauma, but did not know it yet. I felt relieved that tonight it was not my turn to stand beside her and feel her anguish tumble from her heart and spill over into the hospital corridor for all to hear. I can want to make it right for all I am worth, but some moments are broken beyond belief, never to be repaired. In such times, one can only stand by silently and be as available as possible, hoping that the very act of presence offers some comfort and some healing.

I watched as the physician stood near her as he talked. Though I could not hear his words, I heard the new widow shriek in horror and clutch her face in panic as she heard the worst news of her life. Forevermore, her life would be fundamentally altered. Her two great loves, her husband and her only child, were dead. She was a widow and would forever live life without the comfort of their presence.

It's a strange world, police chaplaincy. You live between chaos and coffee and in a heartbeat, it all changes. Tonight was to have been my first ride with the deputy since his injury and return to service. I'd wanted to hear of his trip to Alaska to recover. Maybe we would even tell a few lies. Instead we walked down the hall in silence and listened to our own thoughts.

"My condolences, ma'am," he said to the weeping woman. "I know what I say won't change a thing, but I am truly sorry," he said to the widow as we left. Indeed it doesn't change a thing. She may not even remember what he said. But she touched his life and mine, too. He offered what he could: his sorrow that she hurt so deeply and his hope that sometime she would find healing.

Nothing to Do

The motorcycle lay on its side, twisted in odd angles and wrapped around the steel guardrail. Two nervous onlookers stood some distance away holding their hands to their faces in dread. One paced. The other trembled. Beneath them, still wrapped snugly in his black motorcycle leathers and with his helmet strapped tightly on his head, lay the victim.

The late afternoon winter sky was brilliantly blue; a hint of early spring hung in the air. Already the sound of spring birds, returning home after the long winter elsewhere, promised the return of warm days and sweet nights. Such horror and such splendor seemed incongruous, and yet both were joined in one bittersweet moment.

"Has anyone called 911?" I asked the two bystanders as I approached the scene of the accident.

"Yes! I called on my car phone! Help is on the way!" said a man who was just approaching.

Sure enough, even as he spoke, I heard the shrill wail of emergency vehicles enroute. Already off in the distance, I could see K-479's Camaro running Code 3 on from the west on U.S. 54 and fire and ambulance units running hot from the south on I-35.

I could not dismiss the absurd juxtaposition of conflicting realities: a warm and enchanting late afternoon. Spring cradling the prairie. The wail of approaching rescue units. And the battered and oddly bent figure of the victim who just now looked up at me with vacant eyes as he lay somewhere between life and destiny.

I knelt beside him and wondered what it was that he saw in his mind's eye. I guessed that only moments ago he was just like me, on his way to some destination with nothing more on his mind than a nice evening at home. Perhaps he was going out for dinner. Or maybe he was tormented with wonders and worries which so unsettled his concentration that this tragedy came about.

I felt a gnawing within my heart. Who awaited his return with eager anticipation? Who waited to tell their ordinary stories—knit together even tighter through the weaving of the day's events?

"Help is on its way," I said to the injured stranger who just now lay on his back looking up at the deep blue sky and me. "I hear them coming now. They'll be here soon." I wanted to give him some hope—any hope—even if it were the words of reassurance from someone whom he *had* to trust because just now he was beyond caring for himself and had to turn his destiny over to strangers.

Always his vacant, unfocused eyes looked at me but seemed to see through and beyond me to a world I could not see. Did he see those whom he loved and was wanting to gaze upon them just now? Was it the yesterdays of his life—the sorrows and celebrations which passed by in review? Or maybe he saw nothing. Perhaps he was beyond awareness and was simply floating in the mystery of life waiting to know his direction.

The gurgle of his breathing was slow but steady. Oh, how I wished I could make it better. But there are times in life when there is nothing to do but wait. And so I did. Officers K-479 and K-58 arrived together in the Camaro and I stepped aside to give them space to work as I passed along the bits of information that I had.

Everyone had a job to do and did it well. The Wichita Police Department directed traffic. Officer K-479 interviewed the witness and, along with K-202, took the measurements and the pictures. Sedgwick County EMS attended to the victim. As for me? I did nothing. Sometimes that's what chaplains do: nothing at all.

There are occasions in life when *nothing* is called for. Not action. Not talking. Only nothing. These are the times to stand aside while others work—to be an observer and listen to the deep, dark anguish and to hear and learn from its story.

There are occasions in the human experience when what is called for is the art of *presence* . . . a willingness to stand silently by and observe the sacred truth that life is tenuous and fragile. It turns in an instant and human life is forever altered, with no chance whatsoever that it will ever be the same again.

And so it was that I did nothing. But I saw the wicked devastation suffered by this victim. When he was prepared for treatment and the leathers were cut from his body I saw the impact of the collision on

him and I was sad. I saw the frenzy of the EMS workers as the Code
Red soured to a Code Blue and they brought all their magic to bear
on a losing battle. I saw the troopers sneak looks over to the sloping
embankment where the dying victim lay, hoping that this grizzly
scene might somehow be transformed from mayhem to miracle.

Sometimes it is enough that I do nothing at all but look and listen
and learn and then tell the story. But always I remember. I remember all the uneventful but profoundly human moments: the trembling of the two women who saw the victim; the calm businesslike
interview of the witness by K-479; of K-58's fingers on the victim's
throat as he checked for a pulse. I noticed my own amazement that
once more I saw a life transformed in a single event in a moment of
time with no turning back.

Just a moment in time. Some are joyous, some are dull, and
others are filled with great sorrow because lives are forever
changed. We wish that somehow we could alter fate, yet know all
the while that the best we can do is we carry out our work with
compassion.

Healing the Helpers

I turned my back to the relentless winter wind, attempting to ward off its bone-chilling cold. Overhead a street light brightened the scene and against its white glow, I watched as the thick mist was driven parallel to the ground. "If it drops just a few degrees, we'll all be covered with glaze," I thought. Even the weather seemed evil.

I watched while the nearby detectives measured the space between the burned out trailer and the one adjacent to it. Two police officers stood in silence near the yellow ribbon that cordoned off the scene. They seemed to hide deep within their rain gear as if reaching for both warmth and a dry sanctuary.

First on the scene, they could only stand by in horror as the cauldron of seething flames boiled from the windows and roof while they waited for the fire units to respond. It's hard to do your best and know that it was too little, too late.

"I tried to get in the door, Tom," said Joe. His words sounded more like a confession than an observation. "But the heat was so intense that I couldn't even get to the front porch. I saw pools of melted aluminum falling onto the concrete porch because it was so hot. I kept praying you'd get there because I didn't want to tell the mom that her child was dead in the fire."

Presently the chief backed his station wagon up to the smoldering ruins, got out, and opened the rear door. I watched while three firemen and a police officer carried the black body bag out from the ashes and gently placed it inside the vehicle. Though the wind howled and the generators roared, the deepest sound I heard was the silence of all those who did their work without a word. Sometimes the silence is so consuming that all we comprehend are memories and private thoughts.

It wasn't just that it was too cold to talk, although it was a raw winter night. Nor was it that everyone was too exhausted from their work, although that was clearly evident. I know better. Our silence was born of the horror of our task, and we were driven to the private places of our hearts where all of us seek solace when life turns cruel and our jobs take us to the center of chaos itself and we must walk amidst the debris of human life. Anyone who works in disaster scenes must face the painful truth that all too often, our best efforts are not sufficient.

It is unsettling to know that all of our training, all of our efforts, all of the risks we were willing to take were in vain this time and a child died. We are left with a hundred "what ifs" to ponder. In these moments of dread all of us who do this work wrestle with questions of relevance.

In a little while another officer stopped beside me and said, "I could carry the body bag to the car, Tom, but I just couldn't load him into the bag. I even helped scrape the ashes away from around him after we found him and I took pictures, but I couldn't touch him. It was just like the Oak Street fire five years ago all over again. When the three kids died there, I picked them all up, but I couldn't do it again. I hate this part of this job." With that, he turned away and went back to work. Some painful memories never die; they just fade into the shadows of our minds and return with a vengeance at the next similar disaster.

I shuddered as I remembered my own summons to this tragedy. A jarring phone call at 1:00 a.m. and a matter-of-fact dispatcher's voice saying to me, "Tom, we need you to respond to the Webster Street Mobile Home Park. We've got a trailer fire. It's wholly engulfed and there's an entrapment. Go to lot three where some of the known survivors are."

All tragedies impact firefighters, cops, and paramedics. But line of duty deaths and the deaths of children hurt deeply and last for a long time. I knew that beyond the actual fire casualties there would be deep wounds suffered by all those who helped.

When I arrived, the surviving youngster was examined by a paramedic and found to be safe except for a sprained wrist which was stabilized by a splint. "I don't understand why these things happen, Tom," said the paramedic as he stood beside me in the drizzle. His brown coat was black with soot and beads of water dripped off his helmet. "It hurts like hell when this happens. I put a splint on his wrist just to make sure it's OK until he's checked out at the hospital, but it's not his wrist that's so broken; it's his life—and there isn't a splint for broken lives. His brother's dead and another one's badly burned. He's going to hurt for years because of this. Just once," he said with angry resignation coloring his voice, "just once, I'd like to get here and pull a child safely from a fire." He turned away to hide his tears. "This is just like the Oak Street house fire five years ago. I found those kids, too. I just don't know . . ." and his voice faded to silence. "I know this is crazy, but when I get back to the station I gotta call my wife and ask her how our kids are. I've just gotta know they are OK. Stupid, huh?" he said as if wanting reassurance that his desperate need to touch those he loves most is really normal.

"Seems normal to me," I said, telling him that when my kids were little and I'd work some horrible tragedy like this, I would also always walk through my home and touch each of my children who were sleeping peacefully in their rooms. I needed to prove to myself that they were safe. You're never too big or too strong to not need reassurance that those you love most are safe. We know just how fragile life is and how our lives can tumble from comfort to chaos in the twinkling of an eye. When you work as closely with sorrow as cops and firefighters do, it seems imperative that we make sure we have a solid grounding in our own private lives.

In a while, the fire chief spotted me and said, "This one's tough, Tom. I'd like to do a critical incident stress debriefing when you think it's timely. Can you arrange it?"

CISD. Once we thought we were too big and brave to need to talk about our feelings. The attitude was, "if you can't handle it, get out of the business." So we hid our feelings. We buried them and put on a tough front. We laughed at tragedy. We sneered at those who seemed touched by it.

But we also drank and smoked too much and cut ourselves off from family, friends, and co-workers. We got sick more often than others did. Our marriages suffered; the divorce rate among emergency services workers soared. Some of our colleagues got so lost in the thicket of despair that they killed themselves. Many good workers simply quit and found less stressful jobs. The cost for not paying attention to the debilitating effects of stress is enormous, and this includes physical, intellectual, emotional, relational, and spiritual costs.

Stress itself is normal. But emergency workers are exposed to severe stress and lots of it. Sometimes it is *critical* and *acute* and threatens us right now. Sometimes it is *delayed* and is the accumulation of several critical incidents which build over time. If that happens too much, it *accumulates* even more and has a tendency to burn us out. Emergency service workers are subject to abnormal events but the stress they experience is a normal response to these unusual tragedies. Even so, it can be costly.

CISD is not magic, but it works. Teams of peer counselors with help from mental health professionals and department chaplains are available to help process these dreadful events under the guidelines of CISD theory and practice. These sessions are confidential and caring in nature.

Hours later, I went home. It was quiet in my house. The wind still blew and the mist had turned to drizzle. I took off my wet clothes, got ready for bed, but sat first at my kitchen table and wondered how deep were the wounds of those I saw tonight and how long it would take to find hope and healing again.

Supermarket Homicide

If the event itself was not enough to summon me to the market, both the message and the urgency of the dispatcher's voice were. "Shots fired. Man down. Ambulance One stand off until PD arrives." I rushed to the market to offer my assistance, thoughts racing as I drove.

It is the same supermarket where I shop. I was there twenty minutes earlier. I remembered how ordinary it was, then. Shoppers leisurely walked the aisles buying groceries. It seemed so incredulous that twenty minutes later I was returning to a tragic scene. In the back of my mind, I was grateful that I had narrowly missed having to watch it transpire.

The parking lot was filled with emergency vehicles when I arrived. Red and blue lights flickered. Yellow crime scene tape was being unrolled and draped around a wide area. City officers and sheriff's deputies peered into the darkness looking for an unknown assailant. My scanner had already told me that he had fled and was northbound on Main, so I guessed I was safe. Still, I felt an edge of anxiety in my heart as I began my work. Was he alone? What would I see inside?

Two of my neighbors, a couple, met me at the entrance of the store and held each other for comfort and support. A city officer took their names while they stood beside me chattering in anxious disbelief. On the ground, a shotgun shell lay as silent evidence that only moments before something awful had happened. The officer placed a grocery cart upside down over the shell to mark its place and keep it intact.

As I stepped inside the store, the utter silence unnerved me. The usual market sounds I had experienced earlier were all gone. No background music. No bleeps of the electronic scanner totaling groceries being rung up by friendly cashiers. No shopping carts wheeling along the aisles. No friends greeting each other. Nothing. Only a numbed silence.

And it was dark. Just a few lights brightened the front of the store. An eerie and ominous aura hovered over the supermarket like a bad spell cast by an evil demon. Half a store away, near the office area, perhaps fifty people clustered, shoppers and staff alike. Groups of two or three clung to each other. Some whispered quietly. Others stood by themselves, not wanting to share anything with anyone. All seemed stunned. It was a bad dream turned real, and there was no waking up from it.

In the front of the store, a city officer stood alone, taking everything in. His .12-gauge was pointed toward the ceiling. Though the violent event was over and the assailant long gone, there was some comfort in the presence of officers with weapons.

It was the grim spectacle on the floor by the south door that told the whole story. I walked closer to see for myself what prompted the whole scene, and stood in disbelief at what I saw. There was little wonder why folks were traumatized. Lying before me was the shattered and broken remains of a local teacher who had been murdered by a shotgun blast to his head. It seemed beyond belief. Just minutes before he had been a person. Now he was only an unrecognizable memory.

I returned to the horrified gathering of shoppers and staff to evaluate who needed what level of care most of all. I saw a friend of mine and her new husband. As if to confirm her worst fears she said to me, "He is dead, isn't he, Tom? We were in the background and didn't see a thing. We just heard the boom."

A stranger holding her little girl asked if it was OK to use the restroom, and would I escort them there. "I'm just visiting here. I'm from Pennsylvania. We expect this kind of thing there, but not in Kansas!" In her own disbelieving way, the stranger from the East spoke for most of us.

How could it be that such a wretched event could happen at all, and how could such a cowardly deed happen in a supermarket in front of a dozen people in Newton, Kansas? Was it really true, as people were saying that the perpetrator was the estranged, adopted son of the teacher? If so, what went so wrong that the only resolution was a public murder? It all seemed too preposterous to believe. But the splattered remains all about the store made this unbelievable tragedy absolutely true. And a hundred traumatized people stood as silent witnesses to the devasting consequences of seeing such a horror unfold.

I shuddered as I remembered that this was the second homicide in our community within four months. It seemed only yesterday that I was summoned to the home of a family where it was discovered that a young mother was bound, then bludgeoned to death while two children were shut up in a closet.

Most of us live with the hope that here in the heartland we will escape such ugly trauma. That's why we live here. We want the illusion that in our community we care about each other, and such ugliness belongs someplace else. But lying absolutely still on the floor before me was the bitter truth that there are no safe havens anymore. The world of chaos is as close as the corner market in a small Kansas town. I fear for our future. It is becoming an illusion that we live in a gentle community, all about us there is a violence that contaminates our souls. The bitter truth is that the callused insensitivity that we hear about in other places has wormed itself into our community too.

In due time, the court system will process the legal matters of this tragedy, and will determine who bears responsibility and who will suffer the consequences. What haunts me is the way in which our whole community has been victimized by each of these recent events, regardless of who is found to be at fault.

I am particularly horrified that this violence was witnessed by so many people. It has left dozens of people traumatized in its aftermath. I can barely imagine the horror that so many experienced as they went about their shopping only to suddenly experience, right before their terrified eyes, the violent death of another human being. In the twinkling of an eye, they witnessed a cataclysmic event, and in that moment they, too, became casualties.

We all inevitably face death. We accept its proper place in life's journey. For some, it even brings relief from suffering. Yet it still seems utterly reprehensible and without meaning when death comes in a moment of rage or vengeance as one member of the community steals the life another. When such a deed is done in public, the sin of it all is magnified.

Standing there in the grocery store not long ago, I saw folks tremble in fear. When they witnessed one person willfully and violently taking the life of another, they saw one of life's most wicked moments. In that chaos, whatever security they had in their private lives was threatened because, without warning, they realized how senseless and violent life can become. In that instant, nothing seemed safe. For awhile, it was uncertain if even more evil would spew upon this community and citizens shrunk back in terror.

With her face filled with understandable terror, one young mother said to a policeman standing nearby, "You will escort us to our cars, won't you? I'm too afraid to be by myself."

Some clung to others hoping to find solace in the warm embrace of strangers who might offer comfort—who could at least understand because they were there, too. If the community of those who might care is large, the number who witnessed the tragedy is dreadfully small, and only they can truly say, "I understand." For the rest of us, we mean well, but our souls don't wake up at night and relive this holocaust. We will not live for the rest of our lives with that scene imprinted in our minds, always lurking there to seep out in unsuspecting times and terrorize us again.

I still hear tales of those who cannot find the comfort of sleep; intrusive images haunt their souls. Still others have put the pieces of their lives back together only to once more tumble back into the horrifying memory when an unwelcome flashback occurs from an everyday association such as the sound of a voice or the writing of a check.

I walked into this hell in a local market not long ago and saw the best and worst of our community. It is imperative that we find a way to walk with courage toward tomorrow. We must care for each other. We must not let chaos reign. If evil has its day, we must reach for tomorrow and hold it close to our hearts, for it belongs to us.

Stone Cold Dead

March 2. Already little green crocus buds split the earth and make the promise of spring seem real. But then again, it is *March*, and consequently, the little green buds look surprised because on this Sunday afternoon it's a covering of fresh snow they try to push through, not just earth. Such is spring—full of surprises like flowers in the snow.

Suddenly the warning tones of my scanner playing in the background focus my attention to the dispatcher's voice. "Ambulance One, Engine One, respond Code Three to the county jail for a signal four. Jailer gives one Code Blue."

I push aside my students' papers that I am evaluating and drive through the wet snow to the jail. And I wonder what awaits me. What will I do there, anyway? Will it matter that I'm there? What does a chaplain offer in such a mystery, anyway? Who am I to enter such a time? Still, it *does* count to share the burden; to hear the story; to breathe the stench yourself. It does count to stand close by and be as fully present as you can to those who must do a horrid task. You cannot be *just* an onlooker and ever expect to be a chaplain in the crazy world of law enforcement.

"They're in there, Tom. Go on down."

A white-sheeted gurney blocked my way to the long jail hallway and an ambulance attendant appeared from somewhere around the blind corner down along the solitary cells.

"Hello, Tom," he said.

"Hello. How are you doing?" I responded, only to want to reach out and grab back those trite, empty social words. "How are you doing?" How stupid. No one was doing well! Just around the corner, emergency workers were trying frantically to find the lost pieces of life and put them back into the soul of a broken and desperate man. "How are you doing?" How could I say such a dumb thing at such a traumatic time? My words meant nothing, except that they betrayed my inner anxiety. I stood in the entry to the hallway where rows of solitary cells stood open as if, in silent vigil, they watched the chaos right there before them on the concrete floor.

When I walked up, the trustee said, "Sombitch's dead, Tom. Stone cold dead. Ain't no way they're gonna bring him back."

Ain't no way. Stone cold dead. But right there, sprawled on the concrete floor, the stone cold concrete floor, he lay.

"One, two, three, four, five," went the EMT as he rocked back and forth with his own arms stiff and his hands clasped together on Vernon's chest with his knuckles showing white even underneath his rubber gloves. Then a pause while the other attendant held the bag mask resuscitator to Vernon's face and did what *he* could to help this already gray young man from drifting farther away. But look at the flat, green lines on the monito—flat like the Kansas Prairie. A flatness that seems to go forever. And maybe it will.

"One, two, three, clear! Clear!"

And SNAP! Arms twitch as if they want to move once more like they used to as Vernon is jolted with the defibrillator.

Arms that seem to want to reach out and hold a child in love. Arms that seem to reach out through the gray mists of some lost land in between and yearn to hold a lover in secret intimacy. But these arms fall flat with a SLAP to the cold, concrete floor of the jail because there just isn't enough magic anymore to make them work. Empty, fixed blue eyes stare right past those who hover over him and see so very far away to some other world.

"Come on Vernon. You've got to help us!" says the EMT as he does his best but knows inside himself that his best isn't good enough this time.

The attendant pressed again and again on that bare chest. Another squeezed the oxygen already hooked to his mouth. Another looked again at the EKG reading. So much energy. So much busy life, so much intensity, all for one who lay, just now, somewhere inside and somewhere outside of life. But who could know where?

Fromthe shadows came Andy, an old-time cop, an up-from-the-streets-I've-seen-it-all type cop.

"Let's go, Tom. We've got to find Vernon's wife and tell her."

The truth? Part of me wanted to stay and watch. A curiosity, perhaps? Maybe. But more likely it was because I could feel in my belly, that knot which tightens whenever I have to tell someone that a loved one is dead. It is easier to watch the drama than to be the bearer of life's most awful news.

At least I could say he hurt himself. I wouldn't have to say it just yet, that he was dead, because he had not been officially pronounced dead. But as we drove to the home, I felt once more the weight of being the bearer of BAD news.

I stood in the doorway of the apartment and felt the sadness. I could hear it still, the ambulance attendant's words, "Bethel Hospital, we'll be enroute to your facility momentarily with a Code Blue suicide." So spoke my scanner in all its matter-of-fact coldness. Code Blue Suicide.

The door opened and an unknowing Laura stood there with two kids squirming underfoot like little puppies while her sister sat drinking coffee at the kitchen table.

"Laura, can you come outside? Chaplain Shane needs to talk to you," said the cop. Small town familiarity. Their life struggle had made them almost friends with local cops. Isn't that strange? Friends across the breach.

"Have I done something wrong, Andy?"

"No, it's not that, Laura. Just come outside so Tom can talk to you. We have some bad news."

"What's wrong?"

It all went too fast. I was not prepared. I can feel it inside. Oh, I know outside I must look calm. I've been here before. And I can't even pretend it's not there—that part of me that likes the drama, the excitement, the responsibility, the thrill of it all. I love it and dread it all at once.

But right now, in this moment, it's the dread I feel most of all. It's filled my heart with a foul-tasting truth. I must tell her that her husband is so gravely hurt he may die. That he hung himself, probably to death, in the county jail. And right now, he's enroute to the hospital as a Code Blue.

Oh, but look. Look deep into Laura's black eyes and see the liquid dread already oozing from deep within her soul, even before I name this awful truth.

"Laura, we need to tell you that your husband has tried to hurt himself. He tried to take his life. He's very badly hurt at the jail, and they are going to take him to Bethel Hospital."

"Oh God! Oh God, NO! OH GOD, NO!"

I was not prepared for her anguish, the shrieking, screaming, wailing anguish which poured out from deep within her. Sounds of bitter anguish sloshed all over me; sounds of broken hopes stained me. Grief screams cut into my own soul—sounds of rage because for one more time, he did something which cost others something precious.

"Oh, when will he ever learn that drinking won't solve anything? Oh, when will he ever learn?!" She wailed in distress as her own heart was breaking. And so on and on went the screams and the story.

I stepped outside myself and looked. I'm covered with grief. It's all over me. I smell from it. I could cry myself. It's not my grief, and yet it is. A blur of events: a quick ride in the squad car to Bethel Hospital and more waiting. Frantic, pacing, babbling, helpless, hopeless waiting.

"I want to see him. I've got to be near him. He's got to see that I'm here."

How I dreaded what I knew was to be. Already I could hear the tears of brothers and sisters and friends who would be there in a short time. Tears of angry grief. Anger that this impulsive young alcoholic would do such a dumb thing as hang himself. Grief that a love was forever stilled.

And in the ICU? How can I even tell you that story? Just stand in the doorway of this small town general hospital. Stand in the silence and watch. And listen. "Wake up, Vernon! Wake up, Vernon! Don't leave me, Vernon! Oh, please don't leave me, Vernon! Open your eyes, Vernon! Come back to me!"

But it was not to be. No matter how long she beat on his chest, no matter how she struggled to lay close to him and let the loving warmth of her body touch him, there was not enough love and not enough hope to turn back the clock and put all the pieces of one broken alcoholic inmate's life back together again. And on the crisp, white sheets of the ICU, he lay so very stone cold dead.

It Hurts Too Much to Go On

"This one here found her," said the officer as he nodded his head toward the middle-aged woman standing beside the car in the driveway. "She's the victim's stepdaughter. The other woman with her is a friend," he added as he glanced toward a second woman seated on the driveway. Tears fell from her eyes and she smoked a cigarette.

Turning toward the stepdaughter, I introduced myself and expressed my sorrow. It felt awkward. What words could I say that would take away the pain and horror of finding your stepmother already two days dead. "I'm really sorry," I told her.

She nodded her head to acknowledge my offering and then added, "I don't understand it. I was in the house yesterday and looked. So was Dad. But neither of us thought to look in the basement storage closet. But then, when I went back in to look a little bit ago, for some reason I looked in the basement closet. And when I opened the door and saw her, I thought it was just a mannequin. I didn't think it was her at all. I didn't think it was real." And with that she shuddered and turned away.

Dusk was settling over the neighborhood and it seemed to give the comfort of darkness for the grieving family and friends to hide in. Drawn by the flashing lights and sirens, small groups of neighbors and curiosity seekers watched from front porches. Cars crept by to peek at the scene as if drawn by an irresistible force. Across the street, someone peered through a video camera to take pictures of the house and the cluster of troubled family and friends who gathered in the twilight. "Damn busybodies," said one of the officers. "What do they want to videotape this for?" he remarked in disgust.

I walked up the front steps and into the living room. I've been inside these kinds of houses before. These are houses where dreams have died and where promises are broken. Where laughter has faded into silence as quiet as a shadow. This is a house where, when you breathe, it feels as if you suck in death itself. These are houses with great secrets which are as silent as the walls themselves.

Once inside, I stopped to look about. Everybody had a job to do, except me. Here and there, city officers prowled about, looking for bits and pieces of information which might make this mystery seem more clear. My work would come later when there is family to tell and comfort to give. Just now, I needed to know what happened so I would be able to provide appropriate pastoral care to all who would need it: the family whom I would have to tell, the cops who investigate, and the paramedics who would check the victim.

Though others busied themselves with their work, I took notice of the walls. Walls are like blotters that soak up secrets and which, if only they could, would yield the most telling stories of all. These walls, perhaps, could tell the thoughts and the feelings of the deceased one's very last seconds of life. But for now, they stood thick and silent, yielding nothing except yesterday's yearnings. My eye caught the simple phrase of a plaque on one wall "Jesus never fails," and I was intrigued by the mystery of this message. In the basement below lay one who seemed unable to find enough pieces of hope to make her life work or enough conviction to believe the message.

Across from the plaque on a chalkboard was another message, "Honey, I'm worried about you. Please call if you come home." A desperate pleading by the victim's husband. I wonder if it was ever seen, or if it was, why was it ignored?

"I don't know, Tom," said a paramedic as he walked up from the basement stairs. "This has been some week! Three suicides! One overdose and two gunshots. Kinda' makes you wonder, doesn't it? Can anything be so bad you can't see hope?" He asked more for the sake of the question itself rather than expecting me to answer. I've also learned to hear such questions as invitations to listen to him, too. These are the kinds of critical incidents that wound all who work in emergency services.

It *was* a hard week. No one says it, but to walk amidst the debris of three suicide homes is to walk through the shattered pieces of broken dreams of three desperate families. If you are not careful, the jagged edges of a broken promise may tear into your own life, too.

Or the crying of a brokenhearted wife may provoke a lump in your own throat.

Perhaps the bitter curse or a distraught father will be too much to deflect, and maybe you will feel his pain as if it were your own. To work amidst the wreckage of life and touch so much sorrow is to work in a field of broken dreams. Some of it is bound to wound you, too.

"Hell, ain't no wonder we had two cops go to the hospital with chest pains, Tom," said the officer as he put his arm on my shoulder. "When you think about it, there's a lot of stress in this work." Then as if to avoid too much reflection, he added, "Let's go downstairs and have a look-see."

I know it's absurd, but try as I might, I always feel a silent shiver in my heart as I approach these scenes. I don't like to look at the consequences of a shooting, but I have long since decided it goes with the job. We turned at the storeroom just off the downstairs family room and there in the corner, as still as yesterday's hopes, lay the deceased one. So still and quiet. Sitting on a cabinet was a note: "I love you all. This isn't your fault. It just hurt too much to go on. Love."

While the detective took pictures, I left the basement with my partner. I was sadder than when I came in. With the necessary information now gathered, the deputy and I left. It was time to find the rest of the the family to tell.

Double Homicide

It was spring at its best. That's what set the whole thing off-kilter from the start. Something this bad just shouldn't happen on a day this good.

The rude squeal of the plectron burst from my scanner into my living room and startled me. "Ambulance One, Rescue One respond Code Three to two-oh-three West First Street. Have a report of two Code Yellows. Need beat officer forty-four to respond Code Three also. Ambulance and rescue units stand off until officers check the scene and give all clear. Possible homicide two times."

Simple. Direct. Clear. Chilling.

No sooner was the order given than my phone rang. "Chaplain Shane, this is Cindy at Communications. Need you to respond right away to two-oh-three West First Street. We have two Code Yellows. Looks like a double homicide. It's a man and a woman and the woman's dad found them. You're needed at the scene."

Sunday afternoon. Springtime in Kansas. The prairie is gentle and green now. It's the time between the bitter winter north wind which blows so hard and cold that it freezes your very soul and the blistering southern summer wind which sweeps relentlessly like a prairie fire and leaves everything gasping for breath. But April— that's another story.

April is gentle and alive. April is promise and sweet secrets. April is honeysuckle and little brown rabbits who cautiously twitch their noses in the greening grass as they try to discover which smells are sweet and which ones promise danger. But today, April is evil.

Inside my own body, I feel things happen that I can't seem to stop. Cindy's words turn inside me like a piece from a tune which, once thought of, keeps repeating over and again. "Looks like a double homicide" and "The woman's dad found them." My heart pounds and I know I'm driving too fast down Main to First Street. I can't tell if I feel more dread or excitement. Or maybe it's the responsibility that I feel most but *all* that I feel bubbles inside me and my skin tingles.

The faster I drive down Main, the more I seem to pass each block as if I were driving through deep water, and it seems so absurdly slow. Cindy's words seemed hard, yet full of energy. "Double homicide!" Even if I don't want to, when I pass by the 300 block on North Main, I see the memory of John Doe. I guess I'll see him in my mind's eye forever. How sad it seems. I'm on the way to a double homicide and my trip takes me right by the place where once I worked another "unattended and suspicious death." How I remember that one hot July day a few years ago.

I walked up that flight of stairs and could see his feet resting all crazy-like and absolutely still just down from the second floor hallway onto the staircase. God, how I dreaded that long walk up. I didn't know what I'd have to see and my stomach churned in fear.

"Watch where you step, 606," said one cop. "There's blood all over and the gun's just to the right of him. It's still loaded and hot. Stay clear of it. Nothing's been moved yet. Why don't you come on this side over here," and with that he pointed to the one side of the dead man whom I now see in full view.

An old memory. A two-year-old, dead memory and yet on this day it seems as clear as it was that steamy July afternoon when I stood at the top of the long flight of stairs and looked down at the whiskered old body of John Doe. His mouth seemed frozen open as if he were trying to say one last word, but no sound came out. His upper dentures lay all cockeyed, half-in, half-out, making it impossible to ever know what last secret he wanted to disclose. Still, I swear it looked as if he died spitting out that last thought. I wonder what was that last word? Was it a prayer? A curse? I looked closely at his mouth trying to guess, knowing all the while it was a fool's speculation.

But maybe it was less the mouth and more the eyes that I saw. No matter where I stood above him, his frozen, empty eyes looked past all that was there and seemed to stare endlessly at some point far beyond. I wonder what in the world he saw. But that was stupid. Maybe he didn't see anything in this world at all. Maybe this world was so empty for him, that there wasn't anything to see. Maybe *that's* why he killed himself . . . *if* he killed himself. Or maybe he saw the other who killed him . . . *if* there was another. Maybe he just plain saw *nothing* at all. Maybe that's what made his life so empty. I bent down close and looked into his eyes. They seemed deep and silent and I looked away. It's hard to look way down deep into open but dead eyes. It's like looking into a vast emptiness of death itself. They seem to sink deeper and deeper into the dead one's body and soul and it feels as if one might tumble into them if he's not careful.

After awhile, with the arrival of the coroner, I watched as he slipped on his rubber gloves and poked his index right straight down into the single hole in John Doe's head trying to find the angle of penetration, or maybe the end of the hole itself or the spent bullet or even an exit wound someplace.

I stood there as if my very shoes were nailed to the spot. I'd never seen anything like it before. An old man lay at my feet, as dead as he could be. A coroner knelt by his side, put his left hand in the old one's cold and empty mouth and scooped out pieces of odds and ends. Pieces of the dead one. Hidden parts now turned to slime. I watched in dreadful fascination as the coroner gingerly parted the red, matted, thin hair on the old man's skull and found the tiny hole for which he had been looking. He took his index finger and probed deeply into what had once been a skull and a brain, but which now seemed but objects of forensic curiosity. I felt a shiver rumble inside me as his finger went all the way in and clear up to his knuckle. "Can't find the exit wound. Can't get deep enough this way."

It was all so matter-of-fact. All so necessary. All so understandable. And yet all so horrid, and so insulting. Maybe when you do such a thing all the time you forget the power of all these routine things. But when you see it for the first time, it's hard to not see it for the horrible curiosity it really is.

Suddenly my attention turned toward the rookie cop. He stood as far away as he could without looking like he didn't want to be there . . . which, of course, was the truth . . . and looked at his first-ever dead person. His eyes were locked upon the coroner's hands and seemed to grow bigger as the coroner's fingers deftly probed the secrets of the man's brain. The rookie turned away, looked at all of us standing there in silence, but seemed to recognize no one, and then he slipped quietly around the corner of the hallway for respite and to let his queasy, churning stomach calm down.

You can't look at a dead man all spread out on a dirty hall floor with chunks of his head scattered here and there and not feel like throwing up. It was hot in the stale second floor flat. Not a breath of air moved. It seemed as quiet as a tomb, which, in a way, it was. My shirt stuck to my neck and sweat drenched my back and soaked clear through. A two-year-old memory called to mind on the way to another memory about to be born.

Still, I kept to my task and dismissed the old recollection and found my way to 203 West First Street and parked my van two houses away. Engine 31 and Rescue One were already there. Their red lights still blinked on and off and on again. Firefighters stood quietly beside their trucks, dressed in black coats with bright lime-green reflective stripes down each side and across the chest and back. Their black hard helmets covered their heads. The thick, black straps under their chins squashed their faces. No one smiled.

Neighbors all around poured from their houses and huddled in small groups. No one said a thing. Here and there, folks pointed to the mystery house but everyone stayed away. You could see it in their eyes, though. "Why don't they go in? Is something *horribly* wrong? Why are all these firefighters and paramedics and cops just standing there?"

Their inactivity was an early and certain clue that this is a house of death. I've been around so long, I'm known by nearly everyone so as I walk through the huddled groups of firefighters, I'm greeted with warmth. The beat officer is just walking out of the house. He approaches me, and bends down underneath the yellow ribbon with bold, black letters which say over and over again, "CRIME SCENE, DO NOT CROSS." It encircles the whole front yard, and keeps everyone out.

That is, it keeps everyone out but the beat cop and me. "Hell of a thing, Tom. The dad's next door making phone calls. He's gonna need you. Found his daughter and boyfriend dead in there. God awful thing to see. You wanna come in and look? Might be good if you do, that way you'll know what he saw and can understand why he's so shook up!"

That was it. The cop's words, "You wanna come in and look?" It was all so personal yet offered in a cop's matter-of-fact way. I had a choice in a way no one else did. I could look, or say no. But not really. I know it was not really a choice for me. I made a commitment to myself long, long ago that I *would* look. I *would* see all the ugly details. I cannot pretend to provide care to persons (whether cops, paramedics, firefighters, or survivors) if I have not at least witnessed the trauma. They are *all* victims in their own way, and unless I have some personal "hands-on" experience, I am too far removed to appreciate their agony. If I'm not there in some fashion, it's only hearsay. My decision was made years ago. "Yeah, let's go have a look."

"Remember, don't touch a thing," he reminds me. "Nine-oh-four's in there now beginning to collect evidence. And watch where you walk. This sombitch's full of blood." With that, we walked up the two steps to the front porch, opened the front door, and stepped inside.

Already it seemed creepy. The subtle sounds outside were muffled and a deep, thick silence seemed to settle down upon the living room. Huge hunks of broken glass littered the floor. Puddles of blood were everywhere. I stepped around them as if to avoid something holy. Here and there, books and papers were strewn about. A fight? Some desperate struggle to grab at safety? Maybe it was just the way they lived anyway.

Already the cop was ahead of me and that was all right. I needed the time and space. You can't just barge in on murdered people; you must ease in on them. I knew full well what I was doing; I needed time to turn up my courage. I didn't know what they looked like, and this much blood this early made it seem ominous.

For a second, I paused to listen to myself. "Good God, Tom. Get a grip on yourself," I thought to myself. "They're *dead* for heaven's sake. You're here with the cops. This place has been searched. There's no one here but two dead bodies and three cops and you. Nothing to be scared of!" I knew that.

"They're back here, Tom. Back here with 904. He's taking pictures. See?" From the living room I passed through the dining room, through the kitchen where I could see back into the bedroom. And there they were.

I knew I had to see them first from a distance. It wouldn't have made any difference, of course, except I just didn't want to have to look at them close up all at once. Something as wretched as a murder is paralyzing to see all of a sudden. I needed to steel myself inside.

But, oh my word! There they were.

Inside I felt cold. I've seen the dead before, even gruesome dead. But each time the deaths occurred because of some accident. Never before had I looked at the dead whose deaths were caused intentionally by another. The dark bedroom was littered with strewn covers and articles of clothing. Empty shoes lay silently by the bed.

On the floor, so cold and so silent, lay the young woman. Only a short, tight, knitlike blouse covered her chest. Her head lay back and turned slightly to one side. Deep red stains covered her neck and chest. Open slashes left gaping, raw wounds, oozing blood, on her neck and breasts. I stood there in stunned amazement. I had never before seen anything so revolting except once in an FBI film, and that was only on a video monitor. This time I stood inches away from an atrocity. My heart ripped at my chest. I felt wet as cold sweat poured out from inside me. I stood there as if I could do nothing else but look.

This beautiful child was slashed to death. No one should see this. No father should ever have to see his daughter so violated. No person should ever experience such shame, fear, and horror. There she lay, wide open on the carpet, so quiet in her own still moist, but drying, blood. Strange, violent feelings tormented me. I was enraged that two people could be so horribly killed in such a way, and a gnawing sense of fear rushed over me. Only an evil, uncaring person could do this. No one is safe! I felt a sudden pitiful sadness for the father next door who saw it all and I wondered what on earth I could offer to this poor, broken dad.

On the bed just next to the dead woman, lay the dead young man. His head hung down between the bed and the wall in a topsy-turvy fashion as if it were twisted and forced there. He lay perpendicular to the bed with his legs bending over the edge. Old, rumpled clothes were strewn about and the sheets were rumpled and red.

I was glad I didn't see his face. Turned to the side and facing away seemed to make it less personal. I could pretend to myself it was easier to look if I didn't see his face. What a stupid thought. "What kind of person could *do* this?" I wondered to myself. Bad enough, though, that I saw his nearly naked but slashed body. Try as I might, my eyes could never quite leave the outside right thigh which was slashed horribly, leaving a wide gap with raw pieces of his leg exposed. I wondered how much all this terror hurt. The fear. The pain. The rage. I could only imagine the helplessness that must have broken them both in spirit just before they died. I turned away. Cold sweat oozed all over me. In ways I had never imagined, evil was closer to me than ever before.

Here and there, the detectives made notes, took pictures, looked for evidence. All the while, an ominous silence hung heavy over the house. There is no quiet that presses down and feels so cold as at a death house.

Sometimes, when the shame of human sin seems overwhelming and the absence of God leaves one yearning for answers which remain forevermore hidden, one understands the lament of the one who said once upon a time, "Where is God in my time of despair?" The horror of sin is no longer a theological concept. It is the reality of two young people slashed to death and then unsuspectingly found by a father who, at this time, is next door consumed by grief.

PART IV:
WHEN IT'S OVER

The house is quiet. No one lives here anymore. When my parents bought it, it was just after the previous owner died of a heart attack. I thought to myself then that it seemed like a house where older people moved to prepare to die. I never wanted to live there because of that. That was silly and borders on superstition. But, in a sense, it is true. That's what happened to the last two owners. Both the previous owner and my parents are dead now and the house is silent.

My family was held together by distance. We never got too close. I don't think we knew how. We rarely talked about important matters like how any of us felt. It wasn't the norm for us. I had to interpret beyond the silence that I was loved and cared for. In a way, that probably doesn't make much sense, but it worked. The safety of emotional distance let us stay connected with each other. If I did not experience much intimacy, neither was I crowded. I was encouraged and blessed and given my space. My privacy was honored. I still like it that way.

But such a privilege comes at a cost. It was not until Dad was an invalid, driven from his position as a senior vice president of a bank to retirement and with subsequent kidney failure, diabetes, and congestive heart failure—when his toes were so black from disease that they began to slough off one by one, and when he could no longer walk and was given dialysis three times a week—only then did we really see that there was so very little time left. How sad. We wasted fifty years of being busy and only had one year to share the intimacy as father and son. I'm still sorry for that. But it seemed timely that without acknowledging anything new, we turned a corner and found each other already there: each one waiting for the other.

"You're a good son, and I love you." It was a simple enough blessing, I suppose. But I guess it's how you hear it and what it means to you that matters. For me it was the gift that I always wanted and finally got. Now, three years later, the house is emptier than it has ever been. With Mom's death, the absolute reality of being the oldest one in my family is the truth I know so well. When death is over, the long process of grieving continues.

One by one, we went through each room and searched every drawer and cleaned every cabinet. Piece by piece, my sister and I touched every old treasure of our parents. There was a lot of junk. Though they never had much money, they had enough to buy better things than they did, but they seemed inclined to search out every bargain with every purchase. Cheap trinkets cluttered their house. Gadgets, toys, and most of all, Mom's bird collection. I never knew how this hobby got started, but for some reason, she collected little glass birds. They were everywhere. Every room was littered with birds.

We told everyone who came to pay respects that they had to take a bird memento home with them. Some thought it was our joke, but we meant it as a tongue-in-cheek truth. But beyond the trinkets, though, there were treasures—memories from yesterday connecting me to a time of innocence when I was a child and life seemed so fresh.

I still remember World War II and our cross-country trip on a train to watch Dad set sail from San Diego for the South Pacific. He was on the USS Vincinnes, a destroyer. Not long ago, while in San Francisco, I found a USS Vincinnes baseball cap. It was the only birthday present I ever got him which I think mattered. It was one of a kind and connected us both to yesterday and to each other.

But mostly, it was the pictures that seemed to carry such emotional meaning. Years ago, Dad was struck with a passion for photography and he took hundreds of snapshots. What they lacked in quality they more than made up for in memories. Every place, every child, every trip, every dog, every detail of all our lives is recorded. Looking back through their albums and old boxes is to go back in time. I can scarcely believe that the old Dad I knew when I was in Divinity School was really younger than I am now. Pictures don't lie; they merely set the record straight.

Mom never wanted an estate sale. She wanted us to take everything for ourselves and never understood why I wouldn't take Dad's old suits to wear. She was a true disciple of the Great Depression; she saved and recycled everything and assumed that I would do the same. That the suits were out of style and didn't fit never occurred to her. We took what we could use, then gave the rest away; what we couldn't give away, we threw away.

It is not an easy task to handle every item and re-live every memory of your parents, but there is a healing sense to it. It may be easier for the sons- and daughters-in-law to do such a task, however, for they don't remember all the stories associated with each item.

With the death of both my parents, neither my wife nor my brother-in-law fully understood how important the old Zenith radio was to me. Our whole family would sit in over-stuffed chairs and listen to "Fibber McGee and Molly" and "The hadow" and "The Lone Ranger" and the "FBI" and so many old radio shows. We were together as a family. We shared an experience and it made us who we are.

Saying good-bye doesn't just happen and finding a *new normal* isn't easy. It requires that you handle and process your memories. One must be prepared to taste the tears again and experience the remembered joy one more time as one by one you process each item, whether it is an item of business or a simple trinket.

Good grief doesn't just happen, it occurs because you work at it. It is the nature of death that we grieve to find healing. When all is said and done, our task is to mourn. If there is no right way, there are guidelines to help.

GRIEF: HOW TO HEAL THE HURT

A bittersweet reality for all of us is that even in our happiest moments there is an underlying awareness that loss will come. Loss is intricately woven into the fabric of life itself. There is no life without loss. But as normal as loss is, it can leave us profoundly wounded.

One might think that something as natural as loss might be seen as commonly understood experience, but it is not. It remains as mysterious and ominous as it is common and inevitable.

We experience the pain of loss in several ways. Some losses are inevitable, routine, and positive in human growth and development.

The pain of such losses may still be present, but eased by the reality that the next phase of life holds fresh possibilities. For example, although we lose the freedom and spontaneity of our childhood years, we gain more independence as we grow older. Or in another example, one may "lose" a child when he or she marries, but "gain" a son- or daughter-in-law. Here, the "bitter" loss is tempered by the "sweet" gain. Both are natural losses.

Other losses are the result of external forces which, though a part of life as we know it, nevertheless thrust us into horrifying despair. A loved one is suddenly killed in an automobile accident leaving us forevermore cut off from his or her love and presence. Without warning, our lives are absolutely altered and can never be the same again. Like Humpty Dumpty, we know a great fall and no one can put the pieces together again. At best, we seek a "new normal." But my, how it hurts! The old is forever gone.

Still other losses come because of our own participation in the process of loss. When one mismanages (through poor health practices or lifestyle choices) and pays the price by loss of life or health, those who remain live with the ache of loss and the added burden of anger at the one who died.

Grief is a reaction to all loss, and can be consuming and blinding. Generally, we find our way through it, but we are often left with deep scars. Yet grief is an experience which is survivable and can even be a passageway to a deepened and renewed life. There are no rules which guarantee healing, but there are some guidelines that help.

1. Acknowledge the reality of the loss and the power of the feelings. Acknowledgment is a matter of recognizing that a life-changing loss has occurred. It is not helpful to turn away from this truth or to deny its reality. It may be horribly painful and we may wish it were not so, but if it exists, it must be acknowledged.

2. Let yourself experience the range of feelings that come to you. These may be powerful and varied. You are likely to be hurt deeper than you ever have been before and to experience an unknown anguish. Crying, sobbing, yelling may be a part of grief. Anger at the lost one, or the one you believe to bear responsibility for the loss or to God or even to yourself is also normal. Expressing your feelings is more helpful than repressing them.

3. Avail yourself of the support of friends and families. Be with them. Tell your story. Pour out your heart to them. Let them care for you. Grief heals best when it is shared.

4. Give yourself time to heal. Grief is not an event so much as it is a process. Healing comes in little pieces, over time.

5. Expect relapses; that's normal. Just when you feel you're over it, a memory slips in unexpectedly when your defenses are down and the hurt comes back.

6. Decide to reinvest in activities. After awhile, and probably before it feels completely right, you need to return to some activities. This is a decision of the head more than the heart. The heart says, "I'll never be the same." The head says, "You can find a new beginning, new experiences, but you must take some initiative."

7. Develop a faith and philosophy which says that beyond this searing pain there can be renewal. Christians remember the Resurrection and recall that this experience was one of bewilderment, pain, anguish, and despair which nevertheless gave way to new life beyond the grave. In similar ways, we all can find hope beyond the pain of grief . . . but it does hurt.

8. Accept the reality of the loss. Acceptance does not mean you like the new reality. It simply means you face life in light of the loss and consequent pain and find ways to go on in spite of it. A long time ago, St. Paul reminded us that life has "thorns in the flesh" and counseled us to find ways to live around and beyond the thorns, because sometimes they just don't go away. The magic in this, however, is that in this very weakness one finds the hidden wonder of strength.

Grief is not an event which is done all at once. It is a process that takes time. It may take years. The stories that follow tell something of the process of others who were marked by grief and who are on their own journey to health and wholeness again.

Memories Shared at a Table

I stood beside Glenn at a friend's funeral not long ago. Here and there I saw familiar faces among the crowd, but they were faces I had to look at twice to see beneath the deepened lines in order to identify them. Age and distance changes things. Even people.

Already silent signs of age and illness marked Glenn's body. Oh, there was still a spring in his step, but it was slower. I noticed how he sometimes bent his shoulder. It took him longer to move about. But, after all, in eighty-two years one puts on a lot of miles, and the new wears off. Here and there some of the other old ones looked at me, too, with wonder in their eyes. "Who is that bearded, graying man who looks so familiar and yet who cannot be placed?" they seemed to say. But not so, Glenn. If he was stooped and I was gray nothing else had changed for either of us.

Right away he straightened up. His eyes brightened in familiar warmth. His hand reached for mine and his face broke into a smile as wide and warm as ever I remembered it and he said, "Tom, good to see you."

And I knew I was with a dear old friend. That was months ago. Since then, Glenn's illness has run its course and so has his life. If age takes our vigor from us and if illness robs us of our vitality, the *essence* of us remains steadfast. Glenn never lost his essence . . . that remarkable uniqueness which set him apart as one of a kind. I've known only a few folks nearly all my life; he was one of those. By fate, Glenn, my father, and I all shared February 25 as our birthday. That reality bonded us in lighthearted humor and gave us a common connection. But it wasn't just a shared birthday nor because we lived only a block apart that marked our friendship; it was Glenn's essence.

I walked into the old home on Faulkner last Friday. His daughter and wife were there bidding good-bye to another friend. It gave me time to look about and feel the wonder of old memories. The upright piano still occupies the corner of the living room where I remember it so long ago. The two bookcases, filled with stories, still stand silent and tall on each side of the living room. As I looked about the home, I felt a lump in my throat when I saw the dining room table where I ate so many meals as a family friend. Of all my lifetime friends I have never sat with those who had a more gracious table. I knew I was welcome here. This home never ran out of room or food.

"Please won't you stay and have supper with us?" asked his wife, Pauline, last Friday night. The essence never changes. But it was more than food we shared; it was a spread of memories. It was at that very table where their oldest son, Bob, by his patience and beyond all his exasperation got me through college algebra. Some of my effort and silent tears are still soaked into that wood. I miss that era. Life has turned a corner and we will never come this way again. And that saddens me.

But once upon a time Bob and his sister Margie and I and a host of others sat in the living room and talked. And Glenn and Pauline and Jim, their youngest son, were there, too. Really. A whole family, including teenagers, spent time together. In those days, the TV in the corner was turned off. In this family, people were more important than programs, and time together mattered. Time with family and time with friends. It was a lesson I too often forget. I was welcome there. We liked each other; we were friends.

This time has come too soon. The pain of loss and grief has settled in the hearts of the old friends on Faulkner. We've said a lot of good-byes this year. And it burdens us. But we remember. Oh, my, do we remember.

All of Us Hurt
When One of Us Hurts

"I'm afraid I have some awfully bad news to tell you," said Linda's mother. "Mary's niece, Sheri, was murdered last week."

A stillness settled over the telephone line for a moment as we felt the sadness of this horrid news. Our circle of friends had tasted tragedy before, to be sure, but something as sinister and terrifying as murder stained an already tragic moment with evil. Such a thing is foreign to our world. There is no personal experience that teaches how to cope with something as wretched as murder.

Linda's dear friend, Mary, already coping with her own recent cancer diagnosis, now felt the anguish of coming to terms with her niece's murder. How much agony can one family tolerate?

In the next few days, the shredded pieces of the story were assembled. Sheri had broken up with her boyfriend. The despondent young man, unable to cope with this shattered dream while also trying to face the bitter truth of his own recently diagnosed crippling medical condition, shot her one night in her sleep. He left a note saying that if he couldn't have her, no one else could either. He then found a secluded place in the Arizona desert and shot himself to death. One more tragedy for one more family. All misfortune hurts; but some can break your heart. In such a time, it almost feels as if hope itself has died.

If only we could wipe away the tears. If only we could hold the grievers so that it didn't hurt so much. If only we could awaken them from this terrifying nightmare and reassure them that this endless, dreadful dream was not true.

But sometimes in life, that which is most dreaded and most horrifying is true after all, and those who seek to care and who yearn with all their heart to bind up the gaping wounds of those whom they love, can only stand alongside their broken loved ones and be as present as possible.

130

There is no harder task than to be present with another who knows a relentless loneliness and an unyielding despair. It is easier to flee and find some authentic task to do. It is more comforting to find shiny words of encouragement to offer—to cover their ache with salve. We want so desperately to fix the problem. It deeply troubles us to know that sometimes the care we would give, though well intended, cannot really change the bitter reality for our friends. And what frightens us in our heart of hearts is the haunting awareness that in some unknown tomorrow, we may be the ones who stand so alone in such despair.

Sometimes there is absolutely nothing one can do or say that will change the reality of another's grief. But in those times, if one can find it in one's heart, what does matter is to offer one's own self, and the healing balm of a redemptive encounter and be present with those who taste such sorrow.

Such a thing, though, comes at a cost. It is not easy to care. The art of caring is to experience the truth that all of us are related in our humanity and all of us hurt when any one of us hurts.

Mary's mother later wrote to us, "Thank you so much for your caring for us all. I would like to be able to tell you tonight that we are feeling okay, but actually I am floundering around, feeling like an alien in a foreign land. We love them all so much and Sheri was so full of life and hope and fun . . ."

To know your granddaughter or your niece has died an unnecessarily violent death is to know a tangled web of fear, sorrow, and anger. It is to experience the reality that life is forever changed in bitter ways. It is to stand in desperate need for another to hold you close, and in their very presence, offer you the piece of hope that never completely dies so long as someone is willing to be present with you, even when you find yourself to be wandering in a foreign land. Strange though it seems to be, it is possible that when life is so cruelly altered and one is so vulnerable, maybe only then do we see how twisted is its course and how much we hold it dear.

Elusive as the Prairie Wind

"We lost her, Mom. She didn't make it." With that matter-of-fact acknowledgment the young mother told her own mother the dreadful truth that their daughter and granddaughter had died.

With the words barely uttered, the grandmother grabbed her own daughter in her arms and held her close. "Oh, my dear child, I am so sorry. I am so sorry." Her words fell to the floor in silence, replaced by the anguished wailing of both of them. There are some moments in life too raw for words. Only the groaning of our souls gives expression to our sorrow.

So it was on this day when this family received word that their teenage daughter, lost in her own maze of despair, elected to take her final exit with a single shot from a handgun. With the tragic death of this child came the death of the hopes these parents had for this daughter and the loss of childhood innocence for her little sister who sat, alone, on an adjacent couch. A big grin spread across her face. Not a grin of pleasure, but of a frozen feature, clearly out of place, out of time, out of sorts. It spoke of numbness and grief, but not joy.

I could only look at the devastated family and feel my own yearning to ease their pain dissipate into a great sense of inadequacy. There are times when silence and presence are all that we can offer. Our words are empty. Quite simply, I had no words to give to help them heal. I had nothing to offer except myself. But it hurt so bad, even for me, that I wished I could be somewhere else . . . except that in ways I have not wisdom or insight enough to share, I could not leave. It was more than my job. It was my conviction that I must be there.

Not far away the grandfather sat on a couch with his arms around his son-in-law. The young dad's hands were clenched tightly together and he rocked back and forth. It seemed to me that inside him he fought the conflicting forces to hold his feelings tightly in control so as to care for his family even as he seemed to seethe in pain and anguish because of his own grief.

"She seemed so much better," the young father said as much to himself as to the rest of us.

"She was," said his father-in-law. "You helped her as much as you could. It was her choice to take her life."

Her choice. How sad. I suppose it was true, from a certain perspective. But sometimes the anguish of despair blinds one to possible options so that however real they are, they can't be seen.

All I know is that once upon a time I walked amidst the broken dreams of a good family and felt it all crunch underfoot as I moved from one to another to offer comfort and hope. The debris of broken dreams usually leaves jagged edges and if you are not careful, your own soul will be cut if you get too close. Hope. That was it. I tried to offer hope in a time when hope seemed absolutely unavailable. The young girl died because she could no longer find hope for her life. The family sometimes sat and sometimes paced aimlessly but they, too, seemed more hopeless than hopeful. Hope can be so fleeting and hard to grasp. Sometimes it is as elusive as the prairie wind. You can feel it on your face, see where it has been, but never really hold it. We can face most things in life, including pain and suffering, as long as we have hope. But when hope fades, we are at great risk.

Very few of us know such a moment. That in itself is a blessing. But those families who have had to hear the news that a loved one has taken her life know a sorrow that never fully leaves them.

Oh, but they remember. They remember the smiles which once brightened their lives but are forever lost in yesterday. The sound of a voice comes back fresh and clear in a crowded market. A loved one's favorite song which they hear by themselves in a car brings back a certain memory of the lost one's face. The last note which said, "it's not your fault" . . . only that "life hurts so much that it's too hard to go on" . . . all packed away with other treasures rarely looked at again. They remember the sweet promise when all of life seemed bright on the day with promise when this child was born.

In time, the family left. I went back to my office. There were other patients to see and other needs to address. But I remember this child and my heart is heavy. All of us suffer when one of us loses the way.

Grief Binds Us in Silent Kinship

From my place near the front of the Butler Creek Indian Baptist Missionary Church outside of Muskogee, Oklahoma, I sat with my wife's family for great-grandmother Sarah's funeral. I've been to many funerals and conducted my share of them, too, but this one was unlike any other. Great-grandmother Sarah was a Creek Indian and only a few of us there were without Native American heritage.

The simplicity of the straight-backed, brown, wooden pews and the off-key plunk of the old upright piano set the tone for the service: old, odd, yet dignified in its simple splendor. I knew it was unlikely I would ever be here again. Indeed, I knew I was experiencing a time that would never return. One-hundred-four-year-old great-grandmother Sarah had died, and all about her were the remaining ancient Indians who once upon a time knew another world, another time, but who somehow still tarried in this one and came to say good-bye.

It was the two worlds that caught me by surprise. On that February day I found myself in the gap between several "two worlds": Indian and white; yesterday and today; old and young. All about me, old ones with thick, black hair and high cheekbones were in mourning. The oldest of them had died!

I felt strangely out of place. Nearly everything whispered to me, "You don't belong." Oh, I did belong, of course, and I knew that. After all, it was my wife's grandmother, the very one after whom our own Sara is named, who lay so still in the simple casket up front. So I was family, by marriage at least.

Folks were kind enough. Johnny, eighty-seven, former boxer turned community leader and lay preacher, took me aside before the service to tell me some Butler Creek Church history. He stopped long enough at the back of the tiny woodframe church, just thirty feet from where great-grandmother Sarah lay, to give me a half-minute shadow boxing exhibition of footwork and jabs. A subtle reminder that even at *his age* he still had it. Indeed he did.

But as much as anything, the language set me apart. As I sat in respectful silence, I listened to a tongue I'd never heard before. The scriptures, the meditation and even the music were in the native Creek language. As the drum beat slowly and as the congregation chanted in words known only to them, I felt myself touch my own loneliness and sorrow all the more. Even the bonds of family and faith were not strong enough to bridge the great gulf I felt. It was not my grandmother, not my personal loss, but I felt estranged, as one who sits in a crowd and knows he does not belong. All those people, all those words, all that music. And all that loneliness.

Strange, though, how it is that mysteries change. As the service droned along, deeper than the haunting unfamiliar Creek language, I sensed a new awareness. I some ways, I touched an even deeper truth. It was the truth of teardrops and the ache of families breaking apart. I began to understand the loneliness that comes with the hushed awareness that one voice has ceased to be for all time. It was a sound which I did know and understand and to which I do belong.

If belonging is measured in the familiar, then I really didn't belong there that day, but I learned a truth that all of us are more united in sorrow and grief than we are ever divided by anything else.

Grief is the thread that binds us all together. We are never so different, never so separate that we do not experience the community of grief when someone we love dies. In our own time, we will all lose loved ones. Indeed, the community of sadness binds us all and is our hope, for when we belong to one another in sadness we transcend all other barriers.

Just a Recluse

Seven unopened daily newspapers lay wet and wrinkled on the front porch. In their own silence, they told the truth to anyone who would listen to their unspoken witness that something tragic happened inside. As I stepped over them and walked toward the unhinged doorway, I remembered how matter-of-factly the dispatcher's voice said, "Newton Ambulance. Respond Code Three, three-twenty West Parkway. Possible Code Yellow. Beat officer respond." And then over the telephone she said to me, "Chaplain Shane, we need you to respond to three-twenty West Parkway. We have a Code Yellow fire death. It's unknown if it's an accident or a homicide or a suicide."

Once there I saw a crowd of curious neighbors gathered in small groups, whispering to one another in hushed murmurs. With eager eyes they looked intently at the faces of the firefighters and paramedics who walked in and out of the cottage, hoping to better understand what tragedy had occurred in their neighborhood.

A rookie police officer met me at the front door and blocked my way as I tried to enter the small frame house. Doing his job by the book, he had orders that absolutely no one was to enter who was not sanctioned.

"It's all right, Paul," said Randy, the officer in charge. "It's Chaplain Shane. I want him here if we can locate the family," he said as he bid me to come in. "Watch where you walk, Tom. There's dog droppings all over the place. Poor dogs probably haven't eaten for a week and they are scared to death. And watch out for the cat. She's hidden some place in the house and already scratched the hell out of one paramedic."

Once inside, I looked about the living room. Indeed, fecal droppings from the three dogs lay everywhere, and the pungent odor of decay hung about the rooms giving its own testimony to the unraveling tragedy. For a moment, I looked about the darkened living room to consider the mystery. It didn't make sense. Each window was taped shut as if to keep out all the light. Rolled up towels lay behind the front door as if they, too, were placed there to seal off the outside. Sheets lay tacked over the living room picture window as if to wall off all signs of the outside world. Or then again, maybe they served to hold the macabre secrets of this place inside for as long as possible. Heaps of clothing and stacks upon stacks of papers and magazines littered the floor. Dirty dishes were piled on the carpet and the coffee table.

"What ya think, Tom? Ain't it a mess! This one's a puzzle. First glance makes ya think someone came in and looted the place, tore it all apart looking for valuables, and then tried to torch it. But then again, maybe he was just one of those crazy old folks who shut out the world and lived like a pig. Ya can't walk anyplace except along these little corridors between all this junk. Personally, I think he was a crazy hermit who just lived this way. But the way he died . . . that's got me stumped. Might as well come in and see the old man. It's pretty ugly, though."

I followed Randy through the aisle between the dog droppings and the clutter on the living room floor, then down the hall to the bathroom. With each step the stench grew thicker and the darkness grew deeper. But worst of all, was the thick, heavy stench of old death.

Just outside the bathroom door a firefighter who had finished taking pictures, turned to me and said, "This one's a puzzle. Can't tell yet if someone bumped the old guy off, then dumped him in here and then set him on fire to make it look like an accident, or whether he died of natural causes and then the space heater caught his clothing on fire, or whether he shut himself in the bathroom and just tried to burn himself up. This one will be tough to unravel. Go ahead. Take a look."

Stepping closer, I peered into the narrow bathroom. The firefighter went about his business and Randy began to poke through old papers in the nearby bedroom looking for any possible clues or maybe a suicide note. In the silence of the bathroom, I stood alone, with the week-old charred remains of a burned up old man. A space heater, now unplugged and shorted out, lay against the torso of the old one. In ways I cannot explain, the silence of the small room seemed consuming. I listened intently to the utter emptiness of the place, knowing that not so long ago, in this very place, one life melted from existence into eternity. I tried to listen through the silence to the secrets which had seeped into the crevices of the room as if in some absurd way they might tell me what happened if I listened intently enough. In their own way, the secrets of this moment seemed to drift about the stale room as if trapped there.

The thick stench of old death burned my eyes and seemed to settle all over me like winter fog. Almost without awareness, I caught myself taking shallow breaths lest I inhale too much of the rancid, stale air. With each breath, I felt as if I were taking in death itself.

And I wondered, "What was life like for this apparently despondent elderly man? Were there those who cared for him or did he merely pass through life in lonely desperation, each day simply one more reminder of the silence in his life?"

My thoughts were interrupted when Randy said, "Tom, there's a sister outside. Better come talk to her."

Standing alone and looking at all the disarray in the home was a thin woman who accepted my introduction with passive politeness. "I just knew something like this had happened. I tried all week to call him and he never answered. I called his boy in Wichita and he said to not worry; he said he would look into it when he got time. He was just a recluse. He rarely went out except to buy groceries. Do I have to look at him? I don't want to. I want to remember him like he once was. Please." And with that she turned aside and walked to the kitchen where she poured fresh food for the still-hungry dogs.

There are times when the most any of us can do is to walk through the remnants of lost and broken lives and try to make sense of the secrets that remain. Sometimes some lives dwindle down to nothing but shadows and silence and secrets. And sometimes the remnants of their lives are scraped together by relatives who live with guilt and grief because one they loved got lost, never to find his way again.

What Matters Most
Is That We Are Loved

"And so for all those reasons I must tell you that there is nothing more that we can medically do. I am terribly sorry."

The young mother and father sat opposite each other in their chairs while the physician told them the worst news they would ever hear. The best of medicine was not enough and their child would die. The physician put his hand on the mother's shoulder to offer the only thing he had left to give: his compassion.

If such a grievous moment has to exist at all, I was glad to have been in the shadows watching the young, tall physician, who had as much compassion as medical skills, offer his gentle touch to the heartbroken parents. If it changed nothing, it made the moment endurable and sometimes that counts most of all. Compassion is the beginning of healing and if the child died of heart disease, these parents' hearts were just as broken and needed another kind of healing if they were ever to recover.

From deep within her soul the young mother groaned in agony. There is no sorrow that lasts longer or is more unyielding than a mother's grief when her child dies. It is always too soon. How can you possible hear such news without your own heart breaking? Parents should never outlive their children. Life is not supposed to turn out that way. From that moment on, all of life is forever lived on the edge of sadness. A promise has died and with it so has a part of one's soul.

Standing silently but attentively in front of his mother, the surviving brother was alive and well and full of two-year-old wonder at seeing his parents dissolve in grief. Little Danny reached the Kleenex box, pulled out a tissue, wiggled between his mother's knees, and began to wipe away her tears.

It was clearly all too much for him to grasp. The words were too big. The experience too unfamiliar. There were too many strangers. And both his parents were crying. Neither one could comfort him because the loneliness of that moment was too devastating for them. And so it was that from a wisdom born from love itself or maybe from an instinct that would not be fully realized for years to come, little Danny transcended himself and blessed his mother's tears with his own caress. I am haunted and yet blessed myself by his gift.

Across the way Danny's dad cried unashamedly. His thick construction worker's arms and callused hands cradled his face and he wept his own tears of sorrow. You are never too big or too strong to grieve your baby's death.

When the expected death did bring closure to this ragged waiting a few hours later, Mom, Dad, and little Danny sat in chairs around baby Jacob's bed. The nurse gently wrapped the precious memory in warm blankets and let Mother hold him. Ever so slowly she rocked back and forth singing lullabies to the child. Little Danny stood at the side and touched Jacob's feet and said, "Toes." Then he wiggled them much like I imagined he once did not so long ago when life seemed bright with promises and filled with hope for tomorrow. How could he know that he was saying a final good-bye to his baby brother? How could he know that his mother's tears, in their own way, seemed to offer a blessing to the freshly deceased baby as they spilled on his silent face?

All of life is precious, even life too young to measure up to the standards of productivity and worldly contributions. Even the lives of infants too sick to live with vitality matter, for these lives call forth our best. They summon our tears which remind us that we have the capacity to love. They summon the youngest and most innocent of us, our very children, to find their own way to care for us. And as our children wipe away our tears, we are reminded of how our greatest gifts come from the most gentle and innocent of sources. We see again that what matters most in life is that we are loved. Love is shown most clearly in ordinary ways.

I grieve the death of this child. I still see his long blonde hair all curly on the pillow. I see little Danny wiggle Jacob's toes and I hear Mom sing her lullaby to a child who could no longer hear. But I heard and it mattered to me because I witnessed her love for her child. And maybe it matters that the song was simply sung, whether or not anyone heard it at all. Sometimes it doesn't matter that our gifts are received, it only matters that we offer them in love.

Visiting with a Few Old Memories

I listened as my mother and my brother-in-law answered the lawyer's question about ownership of any taxable property which had been overlooked. Where there any oil or gas leases? A farm? A vacation cabin in the mountains?

We were here to finish the final legal details of Dad's will. Although almost a year had passed since Dad's death, there remained a few loose ends that needed attention and so we gathered for one more time to complete the task.

Seeing my name tag, the lawyer observed "Chaplain at Wesley. I bet you know Chaplain Carol. She helped me through a serious illness a few years ago." He smiled appreciatively and I felt the formality of the lawyer's visit warmed by a personal connection with a friend and his own personal acknowledgment of his vulnerability. He seemed sensitive and I valued that.

I looked about the office as we talked. Sometimes I crawl inside a moment and let the world spin on while I think about the memory and meaning of a particular time. With the rest of the family attending to business, I paused to reflect.

On the walls hung prints of carousels and his diplomas in smartly styled frames. It was enough to be tasteful but not cluttered. It seemed formal but not stuffy. Pictures of his family adorned a small table adjacent to the desk. Somewhat younger than I, he easily volunteered stories about his adult children's current adventures and how different they were from each other. Of course, I understood all of this; that describes my children, too.

"The first week I joined this firm the senior partner took me to the bank where your dad worked and introduced me to the bank officers. They're all gone, now, and it's just not the same," he remarked in a friendly gesture. It never is. However competent are the fresh new faces, when the old ones who were your mentors leave, there is a silence which is never filled.

One by one we unfolded the items taken from the safety deposit box. It seemed almost an invasion of Dad's privacy to touch and explore old papers and delve into the secrets of his life, and yet the only matters we saw were legal documents related to the disposition of his estate.

Even so, to see his own handwriting one more time seemed startling. Once I was used to seeing it. A note always seemed to be around here and there, and in my younger years, he would write letters to me. I seemed unaware that when his illness crowded the life and vitality out of him, he didn't write at all. It was a loss I didn't notice. Like a window back in time, I saw his writing and felt connected to him. I am not so sure I didn't hear his voice somewhere.

But on this day, I saw it all again. We had gathered to do the business of the estate. What we browsed through were nothing more than legal documents, but like so much of life, the presented truth is not all there is. Lurking behind the legal papers were memories. In time, the legal questions were answered and the next steps to pursue were clarified. The papers were refolded and the memories put away.

As I walked to my truck I turned my head into the winter wind to keep my hat on and I scrunched into my overcoat. Tomorrow would be my birthday. It would have been Dad's birthday, too. Another memory. We always had dinner together. Last year he was too sick for us to do that and within two weeks he died. It would be different this year. But life is lived within the memories you recall and the ones you make for tomorrow. Today I visited some of them in the lawyer's office and they still seemed fresh. Even so, an era has passed.

Nothing stays the same. Not banks, or legal arrangements, or families. Life goes ever so much better for those who can look back and smile, yet who can also look ahead with hope. You can visit yesterday, but you can't live there.

Even so I delighted in the surprise visit home for my birthday by Mike who came from Dallas and the telephone call from Mark in Florida. Three generations touched in one weekend.

The rhythm of parent and child touching one another, then moving on, is timeless. There will come a day when my own children will gather and conduct the business of my life. Perhaps they, too, will sit in silence and look back to some of the ordinary moments and recall their days gone by when our lives intermingled. I hope their memories are rich in everyday delights. As for me now, it is a time between the days gone by and the days to come.

To Be Healed, Pain Must Be Shared

"A lot has happened since our last meeting," he said. "Three of us have lost fathers and Sally's mother hovers at the edge of life, too. We need some time to tell our stories before we do our business."

His words rolled from his mouth with the lyric sweetness of his East Texas tongue. The more he talked of his dad, the deeper he drifted into yesterday. With every word he sounded more Southern. Indeed, Rich invited us back to Tyler, Texas, and the peanut farm on which he grew up and the white frame conservative country church he attended as a child and where family, faith, and destiny were woven together. He may live in the Rockies now, but the taproot of his history is the East Texas piney woods.

When you say the final good-bye to a parent, all the old memories come to call and all you ever were seems evident.

"I left the little country church and found one that better suited my theology and lifestyle. That hurt Dad. He thought I strayed from the truth. My ordination was never real to him. I was surprised when his pastor let me read the eulogy. I am not a 'real pastor' in their eyes, you know."

Rich was helped by telling his story. Some aches must be shared if ever they are to be healed. When they are buried too deeply within, they turn to stone and the spirit can never soar again. It just weighs too heavily upon your heart.

But even so, to tell your deepest truth is to touch the most precious part of who you are and those who hear must love you and listen with grace or they will never know the painful power of it all or the redemptive grace of that moment for you.

"Just before he died, Daddy said he understood why I left the church and that it was OK. I had found my own church. He gave me his blessing." So said Rich as he sat around the table. As he talked, he seemed to look not at us so much as the one who both bruised and blessed him. It's always been that way. The ones we love the most both hurt us and heal us the deepest of all. Sometimes, the healing never comes and the final good-bye leaves the wound forever raw.

Across the table from me Sarah sat in resonant respect while Rich finished his story. Wisps of gray streaked the top of her hair. She heard as one whose own story is painfully similar.

"I fly home twice a month now," she offered when it was her turn to tell her story. "Diabetes and congestive heart failure are sucking the life from Mom. I waited with Mom in the pre-op room last month before they took her leg. They weren't sure she could survive the surgery, but she did. She won't let them take the other one.

"I've broken every family pattern. Mom stayed home and raised all us kids. I've not married and I have an education and a profession. That's been tough on Mom. I asked her if there was anything she wanted to tell me . . . any advice for my life that she wanted me to have. It seemed only right that we have a chance to talk that way. I wondered if it would be the last time we would ever have to visit."

Sarah smiled and her eyes glistened while she remembered that time. Some memories pass by without feelings while others hold the most precious dimensions of all our lives within that image.

To know that this moment may be the final one with a loved one makes that time holy. It seems as if such a time will never come, and when it does, it is over in an instant. All the thoughts you ever wanted to say seem to crowd your tongue and there isn't enough time to voice them all. And before you know it, the moment is forever hushed and the possibility for connecting is forever gone.

"She said, 'No, Sarah, no advice. You are a wonderful daughter and I am so proud of you just the way you are.'"

As I listened, it seemed as if I stood once more in my own dad's bedroom while he lay so weak and failing not so very long ago. Never one to share his private world, he said to me with a smile on his face, "You're a good son and I love you."

Sometimes we wait too long to say the deepest truths of our heart to those we love the most. Too soon there is no more time to give your blessing. But if you are lucky, you'll say the words you've longed to say all your life and something redemptive will fall in place for everyone and forever they will carry a comfort in their hearts.

Often I think of the times I have withheld my love because, for the moment, I tasted only the white heat of my anger or the sadness of my disappointment. But the truth is, nothing in my life is more important than those I love most, and no regret pains me more than to know there have been times I have been too slow to say so.

Order Your Own Copy of
This Important Book for Your Personal Library!

WHEN LIFE MEETS DEATH
Stories of Death and Dying, Truth and Courage

_____ in hardbound at $29.95 (ISBN: 0-7890-0289-2)

COST OF BOOKS _____

OUTSIDE USA/CANADA/
MEXICO: ADD 20% _____

POSTAGE & HANDLING _____
(US: $3.00 for first book & $1.25
for each additional book)
Outside US: $4.75 for first book
& $1.75 for each additional book)

SUBTOTAL _____

IN CANADA: ADD 7% GST _____

STATE TAX _____
(NY, OH & MN residents, please
add appropriate local sales tax)

FINAL TOTAL _____
(If paying in Canadian funds,
convert using the current
exchange rate. UNESCO
coupons welcome.)

☐ **BILL ME LATER:** ($5 service charge will be added)
(Bill-me option is good on US/Canada/Mexico orders only;
not good to jobbers, wholesalers, or subscription agencies.)

☐ Check here if billing address is different from
shipping address and attach purchase order and
billing address information.

Signature_____

☐ **PAYMENT ENCLOSED: $** _____

☐ **PLEASE CHARGE TO MY CREDIT CARD.**

☐ Visa ☐ MasterCard ☐ AmEx ☐ Discover
☐ Diners Club
Account # _____

Exp. Date _____

Signature _____

Prices in US dollars and subject to change without notice.

NAME _____

INSTITUTION _____

ADDRESS _____

CITY _____

STATE/ZIP _____

COUNTRY _____ COUNTY (NY residents only) _____

TEL _____ FAX _____

E-MAIL_____
May we use your e-mail address for confirmations and other types of information? ☐ Yes   ☐ No

Order From Your Local Bookstore or Directly From
The Haworth Press, Inc.
10 Alice Street, Binghamton, New York 13904-1580 • USA
TELEPHONE: 1-800-HAWORTH (1-800-429-6784) / Outside US/Canada: (607) 722-5857
FAX: 1-800-895-0582 / Outside US/Canada: (607) 772-6362
E-mail: getinfo@haworth.com
PLEASE PHOTOCOPY THIS FORM FOR YOUR PERSONAL USE.

BOF96

FORTHCOMING and NEW BOOKS
IN RELIGION, MINISTRY & PASTORAL CARE

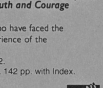

WHAT THE DYING TEACH US

Lessons on Living
Reverend Samuel Lee Oliver, BCC
A collection of actual experiences and insights shared
by terminally ill persons.
$29.95 hard. ISBN: 0-7890-0475-5.
$14.95 soft. ISBN: 0-7890-0476-3.
Available Summer 1998. Approx. 114 pp. with Index.
Features personal reflections on death and dying.

SPIRITUAL CRISIS

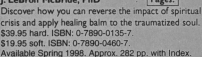

Surviving Trauma to the Soul
J. LeBron McBride, PhD
Discover how you can reverse the impact of spiritual
crisis and apply healing balm to the traumatized soul.
$39.95 hard. ISBN: 0-7890-0135-7.
$19.95 soft. ISBN: 0-7890-0460-7.
Available Spring 1998. Approx. 282 pp. with Index.
Features case studies, tables, and figures.

HIDDEN ADDICTIONS

A Pastoral Response to the Abuse of Legal Drugs
Bridget Clare McKeever, PhD, SSL
Shows you the social roots of addiction and gives you the
spiritual and religious resources necessary to put you and
your loved ones on the road to holistic recovery.
$29.95 hard. ISBN: 0-7890-0266-3.
$14.95 soft. ISBN: 0-7890-0267-1.
Available Spring 1998. Approx. 149 pp. with Index.
Features case studies and a bibliography.

UNDERSTANDING CLERGY MISCONDUCT
IN RELIGIOUS SYSTEMS

Scapegoating, Family Secrets, and the Abuse of Power
Candace R. Benyei, PhD
Helps you see leaders of religious institutions in a way that
the world has been afraid to see them—in a glass clearly.
$29.95 hard. ISBN: 0-7890-0451-8.
$19.95 soft. ISBN: 0-7890-0452-6.
Available Spring 1998. Approx. 203 pp. with Index.
Features a glossary and appendixes.

THE EIGHT MASKS OF MEN

*A Practical Guide in Spiritual Growth
for Men of the Christian Faith*
Rev. Dr. Frederick G. Grosse
This book will encourage you to come out from behind
your mask of solitude and loneliness—one of man's most
obtrusive masks—and reach out for help and community.
$39.95 hard. ISBN: 0-7890-0415-1.
$19.95 soft. ISBN: 0-7890-0416-X.
Available Winter 1997/98. Approx. 181 pp. with Index.
**Features anecdotal stories and excerpts by men who
have undergone spiritual group work and
an appendix of biblical references for spiritual growth.**

WHEN LIFE MEETS DEATH

Stories of Death and Dying, Truth and Courage
Thomas William Shane, DDiv
A book of stories from people who have faced the
ordinary, yet overwhelming, experience of the
death of a loved one.
$39.95 hard. ISBN: 0-7890-0289-2.
Available Winter 1997/98. Approx. 142 pp. with Index.

THE HEART
OF PASTORAL COUNSELING

Healing Through Relationship, Revised Edition
Richard Dayringer, ThD
On the first edition:
*"A comprehensive volume that offers concrete help and
provides ladders for those suffering counseling pitfalls."*
—*Ministry*
$39.95 hard. ISBN: 0-7890-0172-1.
$19.95 soft. ISBN: 0-7890-0421-6.
Available Winter 1997/98. Approx. 209 pp. with Index.
**Features 4 appendixes, charts/figures,
diagnostic criteria, and a bibliography.**

DYING, GRIEVING, FAITH, AND FAMILY

A Pastoral Care Approach
George W. Bowman, III, ThM, BD
Provocative, suggestive, and stimulating to professionals and
educators working with and teaching about dying and
grieving persons.
$39.95 hard. ISBN: 0-7890-0262-0.
$19.95 soft. ISBN: 0-7890-0263-9.
Available Fall 1997. Approx. 150 pp. with Index.

THE PASTORAL CARE OF DEPRESSION

A Guidebook
Binford W. Gilbert, PhD
Shows pastors how to help people who come to them
in a state of depression.
$29.95 hard. ISBN: 0-7890-0264-7.
$14.95 soft. ISBN: 0-7890-0265-5.
1997. Available now. 127 pp. with Index.

A GOSPEL FOR THE MATURE YEARS

Finding Fulfillment by Knowing and Using Your Gifts
**Harold G. Koenig, MD, Tracy Lamar, MDiv,
and Betty Lamar, BFA**
Guides middle-aged and older adults toward emotional and
spiritual growth, joy, and satisfaction in their mature years
regardless of their circumstances, health, or age.
$39.95 hard. ISBN: 0-7890-0158-6.
$19.95 soft. ISBN: 0-7890-0170-5. 1997. Available now. 148 pp.

Faculty: Textbooks are available for classroom adoption consideration on a
60–day examination basis. You will receive an invoice payable within 60 days along
with the book. **If you decide to adopt the book, your invoice will be cancelled.**
Please write to us on your institutional letterhead, indicating the textbook you would
like to examine as well as the following information: course title, current text,
enrollment, and decision date.

 The Haworth Pastoral Press
An imprint of the The Haworth Press, Inc.
10 Alice Street
Binghamton, New York 13904–1580 USA

 **Visit our online catalog and search
for publications of interest to you by
title, author, keyword, or subject!
http://www.haworth.com**

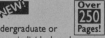